MW00606230

The
Tough Kid®
Electronic Home Notes

JAMES KNORR, PH.D.

WILLIAM R. JENSON, PH.D.

LAURA LOPACH, PH.D., BCBA-D

© 2017 William R. Jenson

The Tough Kid is a registered trademark of William R. Jenson and
Ginger Rhode in the United States.

The purchaser is granted permission to use and reproduce the reproducible forms
in this book and available for download solely for use in implementing *The Tough Kid
Electronic Home Notes* program as described in this book. Except as expressly permitted
above and under the United States Copyright Act of 1976, no materials in this work
may be used, reproduced, or distributed in any form or by any means, electronic or
mechanical, without the prior written permission of the publisher.

Published in the United States by
Pacific Northwest Publishing
21 W. 6th Ave.
Eugene, Oregon 97401
www.pacificnwpublish.com

ISBN: 978-1-59909-085-6

Cover by Nick Siegrist
Interior design and layout by Natalie Conaway
Illustrations by Tom Oling, Tom Zilis, Aaron Graham, and Nick Siegrist
Additional art provided by clipart.com, © 2017 Jupiterimages Corporation
Google and the Google logo are registered trademarks of Google, Inc.

Pacific
Northwest
Publishing

Eugene, Oregon | www.pacificnwpublish.com

To download reproducible forms, go to cdcontent.pacificnwpublish.com
and enter access code: 978-1-59909-085-6

This book is dedicated to my wife, Erica, who supported me throughout my education and the countless nights of working to be who I am today. To my parents, LuAnn, Michael, Lee, and Lucy, who taught me how to be a good person, to persist toward my goals, and to love what I do.

To my advisors at the University of Utah, who taught me the meaning of hard work and the appreciation it brings. And to my dog Powder, who, despite having lost out on many hikes because of my work, reminds me that there is always an adventure to be had.

—James M. Knorr

To all the families and teachers who work together to make sure Tough Kids are successful at school and home . . .

—William R. Jenson

There are several important people to whom I would like to express gratitude for their encouragement and inspiration. First, I would like to recognize and thank Matt, Dennis, Sheila, and Patrick for their unfailing love and dedication throughout this process. Second, I would like to acknowledge Dr. Margaret Beebe-Frankenberger for her mentorship at the University of Montana. Third, I am indebted to my coauthors Drs. Jenson and Knorr for sharing their breadth of knowledge and thoughtful guidance. Lastly, I would like to extend thanks to Pacific Northwest Publishing and its staff for their investment in this project.

—Laura Lopach

James Knorr, Ph.D.

James Knorr is a postdoctoral resident at the Neurology Learning and Behavior Center in Salt Lake City, Utah. He earned his Ph.D. in School Psychology from the University of Utah in 2015. James has previously worked in schools as a school psychologist.

His interests include assessment and intervention of children and adolescents with neuro-development disorders, severe behavior disorders, and disorders with genetic etiology. He is also interested in technology-based interventions.

William R. Jenson, Ph.D.

Dr. William R. Jenson is a professor and past chair of the Department of Educational Psychology at the University of Utah. He received his Ph.D. in School Psychology/Applied Behavior Analysis from Utah State University in 1975. He directed the Adolescent Residential Unit in Las Vegas, Nevada, and the Children's Behavior Therapy Unit (CBTU) for Salt Lake Mental Health. CBTU is a day hospital program for severely emotionally disturbed and autistic

children. Dr. Jenson's interests include behavior management for severe behavior problems, behavioral assessment, school-based interventions, parent training, applied technology, and meta-analytic research.

Dr. Jenson has authored and coauthored more than one hundred articles, chapters, and books, including the *Tough Kid Book, Tough Kid Tool Box, Tough Kid Parent Book, Tough Kid Principal's Briefcase, Understanding Childhood Behavior Disorders, Structured Teaching, Best Practices: Behavioral and Educational Strategies, Teaching Behaviorally Disordered Students: Preferred Practices, School-Based Interventions for Students with Behavior Problems, Functional Assessment and Intervention Program, Get 'em on Task* computer program, and several others.

Laura Lopach, Ph.D., BCBA-D

Laura Lopach is a school psychologist in Granite District in Salt Lake City, Utah, and a certified behavior analyst. She is a member of the district autism team and oversees districtwide autism assessment and eligibility determination. She earned her Ph.D. in Educational Psychology from the University of Utah in 2016 and her M.A. in School Psychology from the University of Montana in 2012.

She has years of experience providing comprehensive services to children and adults with behavioral, social, and emotional challenges and their families. She has provided evidence-based intervention services in home, school, and residential treatment settings. Her research interests include identifying effective and practical interventions to support learning and prosocial behavior.

contents

SECTION 4 • Setting Up Google Files . . . 107

T*he Tough Kid Electronic Home Notes* is a program for our challenging students who struggle behaviorally and academically. These students often disappoint themselves, their families, and their teachers. Through strong support and ongoing communication between the classroom teacher and the student's home, our goal is to get everyone fully charged and logged in for academic and behavioral success.

The Tough Kid Electronic Home Notes combines school and home collaboration, communication by email, automated progress monitoring, and proven motivation systems to create a highly effective school and home intervention.

■ Pop-Up Box

Research

Home notes (also known as Daily Report Cards) have a long and robust research base.

The primary players are the student, the family, and the teacher. The program may be initiated and supported by an interventionist, or the teacher may also serve as the interventionist (teacher-interventionist).

It's Included!

We've included clear step-by-step procedures, reproducible materials (available through online download), and motivation systems with directions on how to make or locate the tools to implement them.

How to Use This Book

Section 1: Program Overview

Read the program overview to learn why Electronic Home Notes can be an effective intervention. Learn who this program benefits and who will participate. As you move forward through the program, the overview will have provided you with the rationale and basic structure for making the program work.

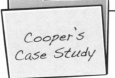

Cooper's
Case Study

Meet Cooper:
Our Sample Student

In Section 1, you will meet Cooper—the classroom behavior problem who very effectively steals the class's attention from the task at hand and in the process is off task and noncompliant. Follow Cooper's case files through subsequent sections as you learn the ins and outs of an effective Electronic Home Note program.

Section 2: Does It Work?

Many school districts now require personnel to show proof of research support before an intervention can be implemented in schools. This section summarizes an extensive review of the research that supports home notes as an effective evidence-based intervention. Studies, research reviews, and a meta-analysis demonstrate the effectiveness of home notes in improving classroom behavior, increasing academic performance, and enhancing social skill development in students. Section 2 also includes research specifically on the Electronic Home Note intervention.

Section 3: Preparing to Implement

Section 3 explains how to set up the elements of an effective Electronic Home Note program. Learn how to assess important student behaviors, select and define objective target behaviors (especially keystone behaviors that are central to school success), and design an effective motivation system. Then preview how it all fits together in a student's Electronic Home Note system. Each part of Section 3 includes essential information that you should read before implementing an Electronic Home Note program.

Section 4: Setting Up Google Files

A user-friendly checklist provides all the instructions for setting up your Electronic Home Note components in Google. Start with how to set up a dedicated and free Google account and Gmail address. Then move through set-up steps for creating an Electronic Home Note and data collection spreadsheet. It's easy when you follow the detailed steps. Once

Using Google

Google provides several free online applications. Setting up an Electronic Home Note using these applications entails a number of technical steps. The directions in Section 4 are written simply so even those who may be technically naïve can set up and run an Electronic Home Note program.

you practice setting up the electronic components of the program a few times, the process requires only a few minutes.

Section 5: Connecting and Training

This section begins when you first connect with the teacher or family to gather preliminary information, get permissions, and determine receptivity to an Electronic Home Note intervention. Next, you will learn how and when to customize the home note and how to train participants for a successful implementation.

Section 6: Implementation

Section 6 includes important information and checklists for implementing an effective Electronic Home Note program. This section begins with how to conduct Reward Days, how to teach students to graph their own data, and how to review academic work samples. The section concludes with a guide for the first week of implementation. A checklist of important activities will help you establish effective routines from the start.

Section 7: Monitoring and Follow-Up

Section 7 focuses on monitoring student growth, data-based decision making with stakeholders, troubleshooting, fading, and conducting celebrations.

References

Appendix A: Practice Making Electronic Home Notes

To practice making Electronic Home Notes, you will need email addresses, practice goals, and descriptions. These brief directions can be used in conjunction with Section 4 to facilitate practice.

Appendix B: Using a Traditional Paper Home Note

When email is not an option, a traditional paper home note remains a viable alternative.

Appendix C: Index of Reproducible Forms

This index of Electronic Home Note reproducible materials provides a quick guide to your downloadable resources.

Resources

When Electronic Home Notes is not the best intervention option or might best be used in combination with other procedures, check out the other resources in this section that may be useful.

SECTION 1

Program Overview

1.1 Plugging In and Booting Up: Why Use Electronic Home Notes?

- Positive in Nature
- Obstacles Removed
- Data Collection
- Motivation

1.2 The Users' Group: Who Can Benefit from Electronic Home Notes?

- Who Are the Participants?
- Cooper's Case Study, Referral for Tier 2 Intervention

1.3 Scrolling Through the Program: How Electronic Home Notes Work

- At a Glance, What Are the Steps?
- How Much Time Is Required?

1.4 Uploaded: What's in the Program?

- What's in the Manual?
- What's in the Reproducibles Download?
- What Else Is Needed?

Plugging In and Booting Up
Why Use Electronic Home Notes?

Collaboration between school and home has been shown by researchers (as reviewed by Sheridan, 2003) to be powerful in increasing desired student behavior and improving academic performance. Research has also shown that home notes are effective in supporting improvement in students' classroom behavior and academic achievement, and in increasing school-home communication (Atkeson & Forehand, 1979; Vannest, Davis, Davis, Mason, & Burke, 2010).

Positive in Nature

Despite the effectiveness of school and home collaboration, it isn't easy to sustain ongoing communication. Educators and families have busy schedules. Arranging regular times to exchange information, even by phone, can be difficult. Unfortunately, without a regular communication system, negative reports about behavior and academic difficulties tend to outweigh positive interactions. Too frequently, the nature of educator and family interactions turns hopeless or adversarial. Instead of a string of notifications about a student's challenges, this home note system focuses on success and collaboration to support student efforts.

Obstacles Removed

Going electronic with home notes removes many of the obstacles to an effective home note program. With computers and smartphones commonplace in a majority of homes, the teacher emails the note home via Google online tools. Reviewing the note is easy for the parent. Emailed notes also remove the following common barriers inherent in a paper home note:

- Entrusting students who have behavioral and organizational problems with the task of carrying a note from school to home sometimes sets the stage for failure. With email, the problem of lost or destroyed notes is eliminated.

- Students have been known to alter ratings. With Electronic Home Notes, the temptation is removed.

Data Collection

In addition to sending home notes via email, this system uses a spreadsheet to keep a record of the teacher's daily behavioral and academic ratings and comments for individual students. Every time a teacher rates a student's behavior and sends the Electronic Home Note, the ratings are automatically entered into an Excel-type spreadsheet in Google Sheets for charting, easy review, and archiving.

Motivation

This comprehensive home note program includes powerful, research-validated techniques from The Tough Kid Series, such as Mystery Motivators, reward spinners, Chart Moves, self-plotting, and participant satisfaction surveys. These behavior management techniques are fun for students and keep them motivated to improve and enhance their school performance.

The Tough Kid Electronic Home Notes also contains a special motivational component (Reward Day notifications) for students. Rewarding students when they review their home note with a family member has been shown by research (Knorr, 2015; Lopach, 2016) to maintain consistent parental review of the Electronic Home Note and consequently improve the student's performance at school.

Notes

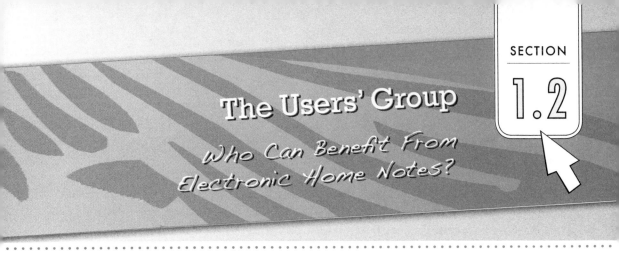

The Users' Group

Who Can Benefit From Electronic Home Notes?

The home note has been shown to be effective for both elementary and secondary students, to support students with and without disabilities, to reduce problem behaviors, and to improve academic performance (Vannest et al., 2010). An Electronic Home Note program is appropriate for students who would benefit from improving on-task behavior, task compliance, and academic skills such as work completion and accuracy.

Who Are the Participants?

Research indicates that 64% of teachers and 53% of school psychologists report having used a home note as an intervention or to monitor student progress (Chafouleas, Riley-Tillman, & Sassu, 2006).

Because many educators have used some form of home notes, we believe the use of this positive and comprehensive Electronic Home Note program will assist many educators in enhancing the effectiveness of their school-to-home collaboration efforts.

Participants in our Electronic Home Note program include the teacher, the family, the student, and often (but not always) an interventionist.

Interventionist

An interventionist may facilitate by setting up the Electronic Home Note program, working with the teacher to define target behaviors, monitoring progress, delivering rewards, and coaching the student. Interventionists may include school psychologists, school counselors, behavior specialists, special educators, social workers, and administrators. Professionals responsible for providing information and data analysis for Tier 2 and Tier 3 interventions within a multi-tiered framework are in an optimal position to implement an Electronic Home Note system.

Teacher-Interventionist

Teachers may also serve as interventionist. For this dual role, the teacher completes the tasks of the interventionist and the classroom teacher.

Classroom Teacher

The teacher rates behavior daily and sends the Electronic Home Note to the family.

■ Pop-Up Box

Family Member

Family members (parents, grandparents, caregivers, guardians) sometimes request regular communication with the school. The Electronic Home Note is the perfect communication tool for family members who express a desire to support school success.

Throughout this book, the term family or family member refers to the student's parent or adult caregiver.

Family Members

Family members review the Electronic Home Note each day with their child and send a reply email to the interventionist or teacher-interventionist.

Student

The student works daily to meet the goals, review the Electronic Home Note with his or her family, and participate in progress monitoring and rewards.

Cooper's Case Study, Referral for Tier 2 Intervention

Due to numerous office referrals, Cooper is referred for possible Tier 2 intervention with Bill James, the school interventionist.

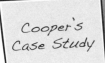

Referral for
Tier 2 Intervention

Student Name: Cooper West   **Grade:** 4
Classroom Teacher: Laura Anderson
Interventionist: Bill James

Week 4 of School
Cooper has been sent to the office eight times in the first 4 weeks of school. Ms. Anderson and Cooper's parents have expressed concern.

Cooper is a popular boy at school, but he is often off task. He distracts other students from their work, raises his voice at inappropriate times, and often wanders around the room to get other students' attention. His negative behaviors distract him from his work and distract others from their work. He is currently falling behind in his academic work.

Referral received from Ms. Anderson
Consideration for Tier 2 Intervention

Notes

Scrolling Through the Program
How Electronic Home Notes Work

At a Glance, What Are the Steps?

The following steps provide a general outline for setting up and implementing an Electronic Home Note intervention. (Step-by-step directions are provided in Sections 3, 4, and 5.) This basic flow is modified when the teacher also serves as the interventionist (see Figure 1.3b on p. 23).

1   Connect with the referring teacher and family.

Prior to implementing the Electronic Home Note program, the interventionist connects with the referring teacher and family to gather preliminary information, request permission to conduct observations, and determine receptivity to a home note intervention.

2   Assess student behavior.

Electronic Home Notes includes an observation system that is used to determine on-task rates as compared with peers and to identify behaviors that interfere with being on task. Also included is the Teacher Compliance Probe, an optional tool for determining how well the student responds to common classroom requests.

Set up a Tough Kid motivation system.

Electronic Home Notes includes a motivation system that reinforces the student for reviewing the home note with his or her family and for meeting behavioral goals.

 Set up an Electronic Home Note.

An Electronic Home Note system is set up in Google Drive. The system includes the home note, automated emailing of the home note, family and student review, family email replies, automated Reward Day notifications, and automatically generated spreadsheets and charts for progress monitoring.

The interventionist and teacher (or teacher-interventionist) customize the home note, selecting and defining target behaviors and clarifying the rating scale.

 Meet with the teacher and family to discuss roles and responsibilities.

The student's support team—teacher, interventionist, and parent or caregiver—meet to walk through the Electronic Home Note process, finalize behavior targets, review the home note email, and discuss responsibilities for implementing a successful intervention.

 Set up Reward Day notifications.

Using an unpredictable schedule, the interventionist (or teacher) sets up Reward Days on 2 to 3 days each week. When a student reviews the home note with a family member, the family sends a reply to the note via email. On designated Reward Days, the reply triggers an out-of-office message customized with a Reward Day notice. The notice is sent from your Gmail account.

Electronic Home Note Form

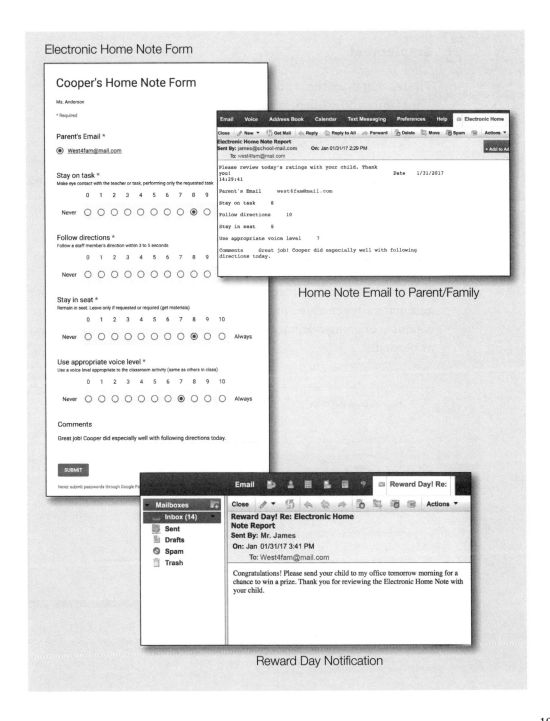

Cooper's Home Note Form

Ms. Anderson

* Required

Parent's Email *

◉ West4fam@mail.com

Stay on task *
Make eye contact with the teacher or task, performing only the requested task

	0	1	2	3	4	5	6	7	8	9
Never	○	○	○	○	○	○	○	○	◉	○

Follow directions *
Follow a staff member's direction within 3 to 5 seconds

	0	1	2	3	4	5	6	7	8	9
Never	○	○	○	○	○	○	○	○	○	○

Stay in seat *
Remain in seat. Leave only if requested or required (get materials)

	0	1	2	3	4	5	6	7	8	9	10
Never	○	○	○	○	○	○	○	○	◉	○	○ Always

Use appropriate voice level *
Use a voice level appropriate to the classroom activity (same as others in class)

	0	1	2	3	4	5	6	7	8	9	10
Never	○	○	○	○	○	○	○	◉	○	○	○ Always

Comments

Great job! Cooper did especially well with following directions today.

[SUBMIT]

Never submit passwords through Google Fo...

Email   Voice   Address Book   Calendar   Text Messaging   Preferences   Help   ✉ Electronic Home

Close   ✎ New ▾   Get Mail   ◀ Reply   Reply to All   Forward   Delete   Move   Spam   Actions ▾

Electronic Home Note Report
Sent By: james@school-mail.com   On: Jan 01/31/17 2:29 PM
To: west4fam@mail.com   + Add to Ad

Please review today's ratings with your child. Thank
you!   Date   1/31/2017
14:29:41

Parent's Email   west4fam@mail.com

Stay on task   8

Follow directions   10

Stay in seat   8

Use appropriate voice level   7

Comments   Great job! Cooper did especially well with following
directions today.

Home Note Email to Parent/Family

Email   📧 👤 🗓 📁 📇 📋 ↪   ✉ Reward Day! Re:

Mailboxes   Close   ✎ ▾ 🔄 ◀ ◀◀ ▶ 🗑 📋 📁 📧   Actions ▾

Inbox (14)   ▾   **Reward Day! Re: Electronic Home**
📁 Sent   **Note Report**
📄 Drafts   Sent By: Mr. James
🚫 Spam   On: Jan 01/31/17 3:41 PM
🗑 Trash   To: West4fam@mail.com

Congratulations! Please send your child to my office tomorrow morning for a
chance to win a prize. Thank you for reviewing the Electronic Home Note with
your child.

Reward Day Notification

Implement.

The teacher rates the student and sends the Electronic Home Note. The family and student review ratings and send a reply.

On Reward Days, the student reports to the interventionist or teacher-interventionist at a predetermined time. During these meetings, the student reviews progress, self-plots behavioral ratings, reviews work samples, completes satisfaction surveys, and is given the opportunity to win a reward.

Monitor progress.

The interventionist or teacher-interventionist reviews the student's automatically generated progress-monitoring spreadsheet and chart, conducts ongoing celebrations, and troubleshoots with stakeholders as needed.

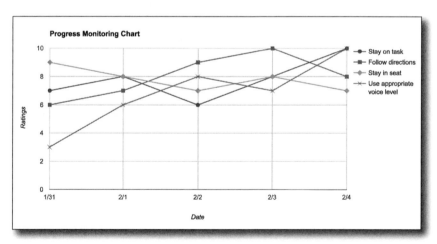

Student's Progress Monitoring Chart

Implement generalization and fading.

When the student consistently achieves the individualized goals and demonstrates appropriate behavior, it's time to consider generalizing and fading procedures.

How Much Time Is Required?

Implementing a successful Electronic Home Note program takes some time and coordination with the family. However, this time is well spent as an investment in the student's long-term success at school. Figure 1.3a on the next page provides estimated time requirements for each step in Electronic Home Notes with an interventionist facilitating. Figure 1.3b (see p. 23) provides estimated time requirements when a teacher serves the dual role as teacher-interventionist.

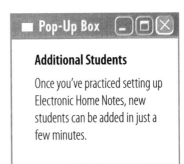

Pop-Up Box

Additional Students

Once you've practiced setting up Electronic Home Notes, new students can be added in just a few minutes.

21

Figure 1.3a • Time Requirements for Interventionist, Classroom Teacher, and Family Member

Participants	Steps	Estimated Time
Preparing for Implementation		
• Interventionist • Teacher	Initial Meeting With the Teacher	10 minutes
• Interventionist • Family member	First Contact With the Family Member	5–10 minutes
• Interventionist	Preimplementation Classroom Observations	Two or three 15-minute observations
• Interventionist	Learning How to Set Up an Electronic Home Note System (time will vary depending on prior experience with Google online applications)	First setup: »1.5 hours Notes for other students: 10 minutes each
• Interventionist • Teacher	Meeting: Teacher Training, Customizing the Home Note	30–60 minutes
• Interventionist • Teacher • Family member	Meeting: Teacher and Family	30–60 minutes
• Interventionist • Student	Meeting: Student	20–30 minutes
• Teacher	Sending the Home Note	1–2 minutes daily
Implementation		
• Family member • Student	Reviewing the Home Note and Replying	2–3 minutes daily
• Interventionist • Student	Reward Days With the Interventionist	5–10 minutes two to three times per week
Follow-Up		
• Interventionist	Observations Phone Calls and Meetings	Variable

Figure 1.3b • Time Requirements for Teacher-Interventionist and Family Member

Participants	Steps	Estimated Time
Preparing for Implementation		
• Teacher-Interventionist • Family member	First Contact With the Family Member	5–10 minutes
• Another invited staff member	Preimplementation Classroom Observations	Two or three 15-minute observations
• Teacher-Interventionist	Learning How to Set Up an Electronic Home Note System (time will vary depending on prior experience with Google online applications)	First setup: ~1.5 hours Notes for other students: 10 minutes each
• Teacher-Interventionist • Family member	Meeting: Teacher-Interventionist and Family	30–60 minutes
• Teacher-Interventionist • Student	Meeting: Student	20–30 minutes
Implementation		
• Teacher-Interventionist	Sending the Home Note	1–2 minutes daily
• Family member • Student	Reviewing the Home Note and Replying	2–3 minutes daily
• Teacher-Interventionist • Student	Reward Days with the Teacher-Interventionist	5–10 minutes two to three times per week
Follow-Up		
• Teacher-Interventionist	Observations Meetings Phone Calls	Variable

23

Notes

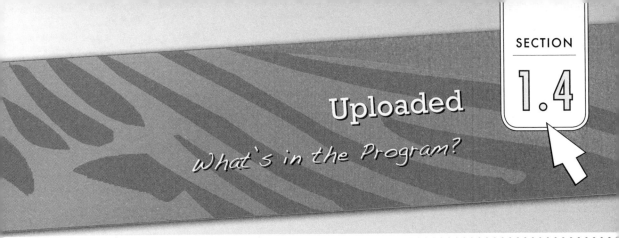

Uploaded

What's in the Program?

What's in the Manual?

The Tough Kid Electronic Home Notes includes all the information needed for an interventionist or a teacher-interventionist to learn how to engage in a school-to-home intervention for those students with challenging behaviors.

What's in the Reproducibles Download?

An online downloadable folder includes multiple reproducibles to guide your implementation. The reproducibles include tools to use with students, the family, and staff. See Appendix C for a full index of these materials.

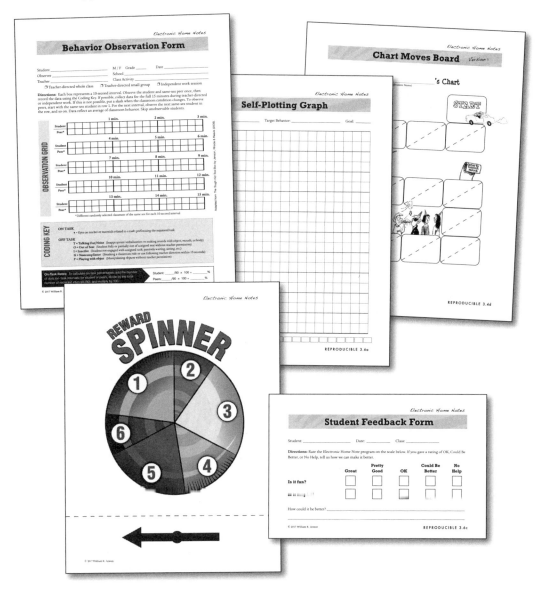

To download the reproducible materials, go to cdcontent.pacificnw publish.com and enter this access code: 978-1-59909-085-6.

What Else Is Needed?

Electronic Devices

The teacher and interventionist need computers, notebook computers, or tablets. Families need to be able to receive email on a computer, notebook computer, or smart phone.

Motivation Systems

You will need a variety of simple and inexpensive rewards for students to earn by reviewing the Electronic Home Note with a family member or by meeting a behavioral goal.

Rewards can include:

- Privileges
- The prestige of a job
- Recognition
- Activities
- Low-cost tangibles

Optional tools for motivation systems can include:

- Spinners

  Make a spinner using Reproducible (3.4c) or access a free online spinner by searching for "adjustable spinner" in your Internet browser.

- Chart Moves

  If you use a Chart Moves Board (Reproducible 3.4d or 7.5a), you will need to order invisible-ink pens. Various types of invisible-ink markers are available. We recommend those that come with a writing tip and a decoding tip. Oriental Trading Company (www.orientaltrading.com) usually offers a selection of markers. You can also search the Internet for "invisible ink pen" to find other options as well as directions for making your own invisible ink.

Section 3.4 provides additional information and ideas for rewards and optional tools for motivation systems.

SECTION 2

Does It Work?

2.1 Engineering: The Research Base for Home Notes

- What Are Home Notes?
- What Do Reviews and Meta-Analyses Indicate?
- Do Home Notes Help Improve Academic Skills?
- Do Home Notes Help Improve Behavior?
- What Is the Role of Incentives and Consequences to Improve Motivation?
- What Does Research Suggest About the Length of the Intervention?

2.2 Application: The Evidence Behind Electronic Home Notes

- Study 1
- Study 2
- Summing It Up

Engineering

The Research Base for Home Notes

What Are Home Notes?

Home notes were originally described as a checklist by Edlund in 1969. Since that time, home notes have been referred to by several other names, including daily report cards (Dougherty & Dougherty, 1977), home-based reinforcement (Bailey, Wolf, & Phillips, 1970), home-school notes (Kelley, 1990), and more recently as daily behavior report cards (Volpe & Fabiano, 2013).

 Definition

home notes

A communication system designed to allow school personnel to provide regular feedback to a student and the student's family on classroom behavior and academic performance.

Why Use Home Notes?

Home notes is a popular intervention that has been found to be effective for:

- Improving academic skills (Kelley, 1990)

- Improving school behavior (Vannest et al., 2010)

- Monitoring individualized education plan (IEP) goals (Fabiano et al., 2010)

- Targeting a combination of academic and behavioral skills (Volpe & Fabiano, 2013)

- Helping both elementary and secondary students (Vannest et al., 2010)

Where Can Home Notes Can Be Used?

Home notes have been used successfully across multiple settings.

- General education settings (Blechman et al., 1980; Galloway & Sheridan, 1994; Jurbergs, Palcic, and Kelley, 2007, 2010)

- Special education settings (Edlund, 1969; Fabiano et al., 2010)

- University outpatient clinic programs (Budd, Leibowitz, Riner, Mindell, & Goldfarb, 1981; Owens et al., 2012)

- Residential treatment facilities (Bailey, Wolf, & Phillips, 1970)

Who Typically Uses Home Notes?

Sixty-four percent of teachers report having used a home note as an intervention and/or to monitor student progress (Chafouleas, Riley-Tillman, & Sassu, 2006). The percentage of teachers using home notes by level is as follows:

- 75% of elementary teachers

- 65% of middle school teachers

- 45% of high school teachers

Fifty-three percent of school psychologists report having used a home note as an intervention and/or to monitor student progress (Riley-Tillman, Chafouleas, Briesch, & Eckert, 2008). Overall, the home note is considered an acceptable, simple, and nonintrusive intervention by teachers (Chafouleas, Riley-Tillman, & Sassu, 2006), parents (Adams, Womack, Shatzer, & Caldarella, 2010; Galloway & Sheridan, 1994; LeBel, Chafouleas, Britner, & Simonsen, 2012), students (Galloway & Sheridan, 1994), and school psychologists (Riley-Tillman et al., 2008).

What Do Reviews and Meta-Analyses Indicate?

Atkeson and Forehand (1979) conducted the first known comprehensive review of home note research. The authors reviewed 21 studies conducted between 1969 and 1977. Results suggested that home notes were universally effective for improving academic performance and classroom behavior. However, positive effects were shown only when home notes and teacher feedback were used with a consequence or contingency management system.

Vannest and colleagues (2010) conducted a meta-analysis of the home note intervention in 17 studies published between 1970 and 2007. The studies included 107 students in total.

Treatment Effects

The studies focused specifically on home notes for improving behavior. Overall, student behavior improved by 61% once a home note intervention was applied, suggesting moderate treatment effects. These effects were shown regardless of the quality of study procedures, suggesting that home notes may produce positive effects regardless of experimental control. There were several key findings, as follows:

- **Student Age/Grade Level**

    Home notes were equally effective across a broad range of ages and grade levels, and they were equally effective for elementary and secondary students.

- **Type of Target Behavior**

    Home notes were also effective across a variety of behavior problems. Specifically, home notes were equally effective for disruptive behavior, on-task behavior, and a mix of behavior goals.

Definition

me•ta-an•al•y•sis

A meta-analysis is a special review of research that reduces bias. Meta-analyses are designed to summarize results of many studies on a particular topic across years or decades of research.

- **School-Home Collaboration**

  Studies with the highest degree of parent involvement and school-home collaboration showed the largest behavioral improvements.

- **Frequency of Use**

  Longer and broader uses of the home note resulted in significantly larger intervention effects. Studies in which behavior was observed for more than an hour each day had significantly larger effects than shorter applications.

- **Rating Scale Construction**

  Quantitative, qualitative, and a combination of quantitative and qualitative scales for evaluating behavior were effective methods for improving behavior. However, qualitative scales had a larger average effect than both quantitative and combination scales.

- **Reliability Assessment**

  Larger effect sizes were produced when student ratings were reliably assessed by other observers. It is generally recommended that an outside observer rate student behavior for at least 20% of every teacher school-home note rating (Vannest et al., 2010). For example, a weekly direct classroom observation may be conducted to monitor the similarity of ratings between the classroom teacher and an outside observer (Riley-Tillman, Chafouleas, & Briesch, 2007).

Do Home Notes Help Improve Academic Skills?

Kelley (1990) recommends that academic targets focus on desired outcomes (e.g., percentage of homework returned, number of problems completed) because this information may be more interpretable and meaningful to parents and teachers. Home notes have been shown to improve:

- Reading fluency, accuracy, and comprehension (Trovato & Bucher, 1980)

- Math work completion and accuracy (Blechman et al., 1981; Drew, Evans, Bostow, Geiger, & Drash, 1982; Galloway & Sheridan, 1994)

- Homework completion (Dougherty & Dougherty, 1977)

- In-class academic productivity (Jurbergs, Palcic, & Kelley, 2007)

Do Home Notes Help Improve Behavior?

Home notes have been effective for:

- Increasing on-task behavior (Jurbergs, Palcic, & Kelley, 2007, 2010)

- Increasing compliance and classroom rule following (Leach & Byrne, 1986; McCain & Kelley, 1993; Schumaker, Hovell, & Sherman, 1977)

- Reducing talk-outs (Dougherty & Dougherty, 1977)

- Reducing tantrums (McGoey, Prodan, & Condit, 2007)

- Reducing incidents of aggression (Budd et al., 1981)

What Is the Role of Incentives and Consequences to Improve Motivation?

A system of incentives and consequences is a necessary aspect of any home note intervention in order to produce meaningful behavioral change. In their literature review, Atkeson and Forehand (1979) found that teacher feedback to parents and students was effective only when it was linked with consequences. Similarly, Jurbergs, Palcic, and Kelley (2010) found that when home notes were used with a motivation system, it produced significantly higher rates of on-task behavior than home notes used without a motivational system. In general, the consistency with which consequences are delivered is highly predictive of improved outcomes (Volpe & Fabiano, 2013). Thus, it appears that home note effectiveness relies heavily on a well-developed and sufficiently motivating contingency management system. Overall, it is recommended that home-based consequences either be replaced by, or serve as a supplement to, existing school-based consequences. It is important to use school-based consequences regardless of the level of parent involvement (Johnson, 2008; Owens et al., 2012).

What Does Research Suggest About the Length of the Intervention?

Home notes should be used consistently for at least 2 months with data-based decision making to determine the need for fading, altering, or discontinuing the program (Owens et al., 2012).

■ Pop-Up Box

Research

The effectiveness of a home note relies heavily on a well-developed and sufficiently motivating contingency management system.

Notes

Application

The Evidence Behind Electronic Home Notes

Study 1

Knorr (2015) conducted the first study to specifically examine Electronic Home Notes. The goal of the study was to increase both on-task behavior and parent review of the Electronic Home Note. The study was completed with four students at two public elementary schools. On-task behavior was not directly reinforced. The study included procedures described in *The Tough Kid Electronic Home Notes*: use of the Electronic Home Note, Reward Day notifications, and Reward Days, including the Self-Plotting Graph, Rewards Menu, reward spinner, and Mystery Motivator.

Participating students were in grades 3–5 and had lower rates of on-task behavior than their classroom peers. One student was identified as having a learning disability, and three students were diagnosed with attention deficit/hyperactivity disorder (ADHD). Every day, teachers submitted Electronic Home Notes based on the students' behavior while completing math worksheets during an independent work time. These ratings and feedback were automatically emailed to parents every day. Parents were asked to review the Electronic Home Note information with their child at home and to send a basic reply email confirming that the information had been reviewed.

Twice per week, students engaged in feedback sessions similar to the Reward Days presented in this book. During the feedback sessions, students met individually with the researcher to review and self-plot their

Electronic Home Note ratings, receive coaching and feedback on their behavior, and earn prizes for having reviewed the Electronic Home Note with a parent. The students were not directly reinforced for their behavioral improvements.

Each student was also observed in their general education classroom by independent observers who recorded their on-task behavior during the independent math work time. These observations were then compared with the on-task behavior of peers in the classroom and with the teacher's ratings on the Electronic Home Notes.

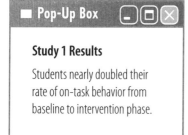

Pop-Up Box

Study 1 Results

Students nearly doubled their rate of on-task behavior from baseline to intervention phase.

Intervention Results

The students nearly doubled their rates of on-task behavior from the baseline to the intervention phase (see Figure 2.2a).

The average baseline rate of on-task behavior was 33%. After implementing the Electronic Home Notes intervention, participants' rates of on-task behavior rose to an average of 64%, an increase of 31 percentage points. The average nonoverlap of all pairs (NAP) value was .88, suggesting large intervention effects. Moderate effects were shown in participants' math work completion and items completed correctly.

Teachers' ratings on the Electronic Home Notes were significantly and positively correlated with direct classroom observations, indicating that teachers were able to accurately rate student performance using the Electronic Home Note. Parents reviewed the Electronic Home Note data an average of 84% of the time, suggesting consistent review. The intervention was found to be acceptable to teachers, parents, and students according to responses on satisfaction questionnaires. In addition, students rated the Reward Day sessions as both enjoyable and useful throughout the study.

Figure 2.2a • Study 1 Results for On-Task Behavior

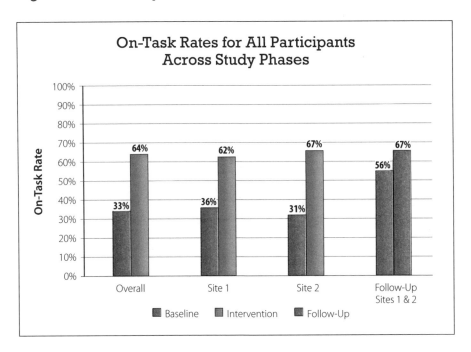

Follow-Up Results

A 2-week follow-up showed that improvements in on-task behavior, math problem completion, and math problems completed correctly were maintained.

Study 2

Lopach (2016) conducted a study to further evaluate the effectiveness of Electronic Home Notes. The goal of the study was to increase on-task behavior, academic performance, and school-home collaboration. Both on-task behavior and parent review of the Electronic Home Notes were directly reinforced. The study was completed with four students at one public elementary school. The school comprised primarily ethnic minority students from low-income backgrounds. The study included all of the procedures included in *The Tough Kid Electronic Home Notes*: use of the Electronic Home Note, Reward Day notifications, and Reward Days, including the Chart Moves Board, Rewards Menu, reward spinner, and Mystery Motivator.

Participating students were in fourth or fifth grade and had lower rates of on-task behavior and math performance than their classroom peers. One student received itinerant speech services and was diagnosed with attention deficit/hyperactivity disorder (ADHD). Teachers, parents, and students engaged in a program training and consultation session before implementing the program, and students had the pre-specified goal of on-task behavior for their Electronic Home Note ratings.

Every day, teachers submitted Electronic Home Notes based on the students' performance while completing math worksheets during an independent work time. Teacher ratings and feedback on the Electronic Home Note were automatically emailed to parents every day. Parents were asked to review the Electronic Home Note with their child at home and to send a basic reply email confirming that the information had been reviewed.

Approximately three times per week, students engaged in Reward Day feedback sessions. Students were directly reinforced for on-task behavior and parent review of the Electronic Home Note. On Reward Days, students met individually with a researcher to review their Electronic Home Note ratings, graph progress, earn prizes, and receive coaching and feedback on their behavior. Students who either met their goal or had their parent review the Electronic Home Note made a chart move toward earning a highly desirable prize. (A chart move functions like a point within an unpredictable reward system. See Section 3.4 for more details).

Each student was also observed in the general education classroom by independent observers who recorded the student's on-task behavior during the independent math work time. These observations were compared with the on-task behavior of peers in the classroom and with the teacher's ratings on the Electronic Home Note.

Intervention Results

Participants nearly doubled their rates of on-task behavior from the baseline to the intervention phase (see Figure 2.2b).

The average baseline rate of on-task behavior was 40%. During the intervention phase, participants' rates of on-task behavior increased by 33 percentage points to an average of 73%, which was similar to that of their classroom peers. The average Tau-U value was .90, which indicates very large intervention effects.

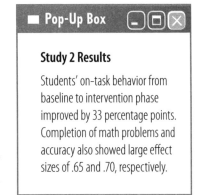

Pop-Up Box

Study 2 Results

Students' on-task behavior from baseline to intervention phase improved by 33 percentage points. Completion of math problems and accuracy also showed large effect sizes of .65 and .70, respectively.

On average, participants increased the number of math problems they completed during an independent work time. The average number of math problems completed increased from 31 during the baseline phase to 49 during the intervention phase. The average Tau-U value was .65, indicating large intervention effects for math work completion. The average number of math problems completed correctly increased from 25 during the baseline phase to 40 during the intervention phase. For math accuracy, the average Tau-U value was .70, indicating large intervention effects for accuracy as well.

Teacher ratings on the Electronic Home Notes were significantly and positively correlated with direct classroom observations. Parents reviewed the Electronic Home Note data an average of 84% of the time, suggesting consistent review. The intervention was acceptable to teachers, parents, and students according to responses on satisfaction questionnaires and students rated the Reward Day sessions as both highly enjoyable and useful throughout the study.

Figure 2.2b • Study 2 Results for On-Task Behavior

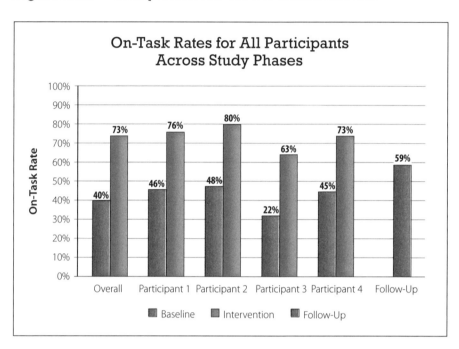

Follow-Up Results

Improvements in on-task behavior were maintained at a 3-week follow-up.

Summing It Up

Decades of research suggest that home notes are effective for improving classroom behavior and academic performance. *The Tough Kid Electronic Home Notes* intervention has demonstrated effectiveness for increasing on-task behavior, academic performance, and school-home collaboration. Research also demonstrates that the Electronic Home Notes intervention and its components are acceptable to parents, teachers, and students.

SECTION 3

Preparing to Implement

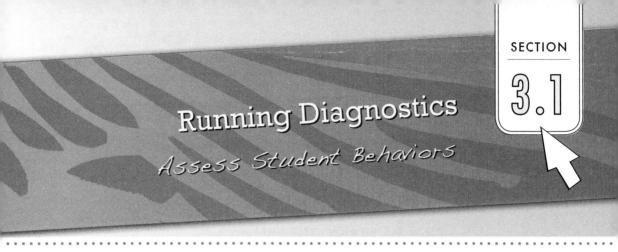

Running Diagnostics

Assess Student Behaviors

S taying on task and following directions are vitally important student behaviors that you may wish to assess before beginning the intervention. Pre-intervention data provide information for goal setting and progress monitoring. We have included two structured assessment methods for measuring students' abilities in these areas—the Behavior Observation Form (Jenson & Sprick, 2014) and the Teacher Compliance Probe Checklist (Rhode, Jenson, & Reavis, 2010).

Objectives

To provide tools for:

- Assessing on-task behavior
- Assessing compliance (following directions)

How to Conduct Observations

Use the Behavior Observation Form (Reproducible 3.1a) during two or three 15-minute classroom observations. Each observation is a 15-minute momentary sampling period with 90 10-second observation intervals. This system assesses time on task and the frequency of talking out, out of seat, inactivity, and playing with objects. In addition, this system collects on-task data for peers to determine how the referred student's time on task compares with peers. Optionally, the teacher may wish to assess the teacher's ratio of positive interactions to negative interactions. These data can be used to help the teacher maintain or develop a classroom climate that supports positive student behavior.

Who Conducts the Observations?

If an interventionist is facilitating the intervention, usually that staff member conducts the observations. If a teacher-interventionist is running the home note program, another staff member will need to conduct the observations.

Materials Preparation

Schedule

Two or three observation periods with the classroom teacher and interventionist or outside observer

Program Materials

Behavior Observation Form (Reproducible 3.1a)

Additional Items

- A timing device that can be set to 10-second intervals (the timer should not be loud or disruptive in any way)
- Pencil

Reproducible forms are available to download.

Guideline

Generally, students who are observed to be on task 60% of the time or less are good candidates for an on-task goal. **NOTE:** If peers' on-task rate is lower than 80%, the teacher may wish to explore options for improving on-task behavior classwide. (See Resources at the end of the book.)

Using the Behavior Observation Form

Use the Behavior Observation Form to record behavior during each observation. Figure 3.1a on the next page shows a completed observation form. Use the definitions of on-task and off-task behavior shown below. These definitions are included on the form.

Definitions

on task

1) Maintaining eye contact with the teacher or task, and
2) Performing the requested task.

off task

Talking out, making noise, out of seat, inactive, noncompliant, playing with an object during class time.

About the Form

Each row on the form provides space to record 3 minutes' worth of on/off-task behavior. Each minute is divided into six boxes, with each box representing a 10-second interval.

The top row of each 3-minute section (see below) provides spaces to record on- or off-task data for the referred student. The bottom row provides spaces to record on- or off-task data for same-sex peers.

						1 min.						2 min.						3 min.
Student																		
Peer*																		

Figure 3.1a • Behavior Observation Form

Electronic Home Notes

Behavior Observation Form

Student _Cooper_ Ⓜ F Grade _2_ Date _11/18_
Observer _Mr. Carlisle_ School _Jefferson Elementary_
Teacher _Ms. Anderson_ Class Activity _____
❏ Teacher-directed whole class ❏ Teacher-directed small group ☒ Independent work session

Directions: Each box represents a 10-second interval. Observe the student and same-sex peer once, then record the data using the Coding Key. If possible, collect data for the full 15 minutes during teacher-directed or independent work. If this is not possible, put a slash when the classroom condition changes. To observe peers, start with the same-sex student in row 1. For the next interval, observe the next same-sex student in the row, and so on. Data reflect an average of classroom behavior. Skip unobservable students.

OBSERVATION GRID

	1 min.					2 min.					3 min.			
Student	.	.	T	T	T	O	O	O	O	O	.	.	.	.	N	N	N	N
Peer*	.	.	.	.	.	.	.	.	.	.	.	.	.	.	I	I	I	.

	4 min.					5 min.					6 min.			
Student	N	N	.	.	.	.	.	O	O	.	.	.	.	.	T	T	T	T
Peer*	.	.	.	.	.	.	I	T	N	.	.	.	.	N	N	.	.	.

	7 min.					8 min.					9 min.			
Student	T	.	.	.	.	.	.	.	.	.	T	T	T	T	T	T
Peer*	.	.	O	O	O	.	.	.	.	.	.	.	.	.	.	.

	10 min.					11 min.					12 min.			
Student	T	.	.	.	.	.	N	N	N	N	N	N	.	.	.	.	.	.
Peer*	P	P	.	.	.	.	.	.	.	T	.	.	.	.	.	.

	13 min.					14 min.					15 min.			
Student	O	O	O	O	O	O	.	.	.	.	.	.	.	.	T	T	T	T
Peer*	I	I	.	.	.	O	.	.	.	P	.	.	.	.	.	.

*Different randomly selected classmate of the same sex for each 10-second interval

Adapted from *The Tough Kid Tool Box* by Jenson, Rhode & Reavis (2009).

CODING KEY

ON TASK
  • = Eyes on teacher or materials related to a task; performing the requested task

OFF TASK
  T = **Talking Out/Noise** (Inappropriate verbalization or making sounds with object, mouth, or body)
  O = **Out of Seat** (Student fully or partially out of assigned seat without teacher permission)
  I = **Inactive** (Student not engaged with assigned task; passively waiting, sitting, etc.)
  N = **Noncompliance** (Breaking a classroom rule or not following teacher direction within 15 seconds)
  P = **Playing with object** (Manipulating objects without teacher permission)

On-Task Rates: To calculate on-task percentages, add the number of dots (on-task intervals) for student or peers, divide by the total number of recorded intervals (90), and multiply by 100.

Student: _45_/90 × 100 = _50_ %
Peers: _72_/90 × 100 = _80_ %

© 2017 William R. Jenson REPRODUCIBLE 3.1a

Steps for Completing the Observation

1. **Fill in the referred student's identification information and other school information.**

2. **Position yourself so you can easily observe the referred student and a number of same-sex peers simultaneously.**

   Observe in the least conspicuous manner possible. It is often best to sit near the back of the classroom with a clear view of the student.

3. **Indicate the class activity that students are engaged in and check the appropriate instructional grouping arrangement box.**

   Examples of class activities include reading group, math worksheets, science lab, and reading with a partner. Check one of the instructional grouping arrangement boxes—teacher-directed whole class, teacher-directed small group, or independent work. If possible, collect data for the full 15 minutes under one work condition. If this is not possible, put a slash when the classroom condition changes and note relevant details about the shift in activity or grouping arrangement.

4. **Start the observation and your timer.**

5a. **For the first 10-second interval, in the first box record on-task/off-task behavior for the referred student.**

   If the target student is on task (i.e., making eye contact with the teacher or performing the required task) for the entire 10-second interval, put a dot (•) in the box.

   If the target student is off task during any part of the 10-second interval, mark the appropriate code in the box (see Box 3.1a on the next page or refer to the Coding Key on the Behavior Observation Form).

Box 3.1a

Behavior Observation Form
Coding Key

On Task = • (dot)

Making eye contact with the teacher or performing the required task for the entire 10-second interval

Off Task

T = Talking Out/Noise

Inappropriate verbalization or making sounds with object, mouth, or body

O = Out of Seat

Student fully or partially out of assigned seat without teacher permission

I = Inactive

Student not engaged with assigned task and passively waiting, sitting, etc.

N = Noncompliance

Breaking a classroom rule or not following teacher directions within 15 seconds

P = Playing With an Object

Manipulating objects without teacher permission

Record only one off-task behavior in any one interval (i.e., ignore other off-task behaviors that occur during the 10-second interval).

5b. Simultaneously observe a randomly selected same-sex peer for comparative data. Record the peer's on-task/off-task behavior in the box directly below the one for the referred student.

First, select a same-sex peer sitting in the same row or at the same table as the referred student. Record the peer's on-task/off-task behavior using the same procedures as for the referred student. For subsequent intervals, systematically progress from observing one same-sex peer to the next for the peer comparison data.

6. Repeat the process for all 90 10-second intervals to complete the full 15-minute observation.

7. Calculate the percentage of time the referred student was on task.

For a full 15-minute observation, divide the number of on task marks by 90 (total number of intervals) and multiply by 100.

> ___ # of on-task intervals ÷ 90 = ___ x 100 =
> ___ % of time on task

For observations of shorter duration, divide the number of on-task marks by the total number of intervals observed and multiply by 100.

> ___ # of on-task intervals ÷ ___ # of intervals observed
> = ___ x 100 = ___ % of time on task

8. Calculate the percentage of time peers were on task.

Repeat the calculation in Step 7 for same-sex peer data to obtain a comparison percentage of time on task.

After the initial observation, you will complete one or two more observations for a total of two to three observations for the student. You will then average the percentages of on-task behavior for the referred student and peers across the two or three observations. This gives a more accurate sample of the referred student's on-task behavior and the peer norm than a single observation. See "How to Average On-Task Percentages Across Observations" below for instructions.

Once observations are complete, share data with the classroom teacher and/or family. (See Section 5.)

How to . . .
AVERAGE ON-TASK PERCENTAGES ACROSS OBSERVATIONS

Referred Student Average Percentage

Sum the referred student's on-task percentage from each observation. For example, for three observations: 65% + 72% + 55% = 192. Then divide by the total number of observations: 192 ÷ 3 = 64%.

Peers Average Percentage

Repeat the calculation above for the peer student data.

NOTE: Make sure all observations have the same number of intervals.

Cooper's Case Study, Observation Results

Ms. Anderson, Cooper's teacher, is happy to have Mr. James, the interventionist, observe in her classroom. She wonders if she has lost her objectivity and is also interested to see how the class as a whole performs. Figure 3.1a (p. 50) includes data from one of the observations.

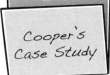
Cooper's Case Study

Classroom Observation Results

Brief meeting with Ms. Anderson: observations scheduled

Call with Mrs. West: Verbal permission given to observe, expressed interest in Electronic Home Notes, email: West4fam@mail.com

Observation Summary (Observation forms in file)
During math independent work, Cooper averaged an on-task rate of 50% as compared with 80% for his peers.

Off-task behaviors included: not consistently following directions, being out of his seat inappropriately, and talking out loudly.

How to Assess Compliance

Another assessment tool is the Teacher Compliance Probe Checklist (Rhode, et al., 2010). This tool provides a reliable method for easily assessing a student's overall compliance. This checklist includes nineteen of the most common requests teachers make in the classroom.

Figure 3.1b • Teacher Compliance Probe

Electronic Home Notes

Teacher Compliance Probe

The teacher gives a request, waits 10 seconds, and marks "yes" or "no" to indicate whether or not the student started the requested behavior. It is important (1) not to repeat the request, (2) not to reward the student with deals for compliance, (3) to act natural after the request, and (4) to wait the full 10 seconds before acting or repeating the request.

Mark after 10-second wait

1. Please sit down.	(Y)	N
2. Line up at the door.	Y	(N)
3. Put your books away.	Y	(N)
4. Bring your assignment to my desk.	(Y)	N
5. Be quiet.	Y	N
6. Look at me.	Y	N
7. Come here.	Y	N
8. Get out a pencil and paper.	(Y)	N
9. Write your name on the paper.	Y	N
10. Get busy on your assignment.	Y	(N)
11. Walk.	Y	N
12. Look up front.	Y	N
13. Come inside the room.	Y	N
14. Sit down.	(Y)	(N)
15. Go to your desk.	Y	N
16. Give me the pencil (or other object).	Y	N.
17. Sit up.	Y	(N) X 2
18. Go to (*place*).	Y	N
19. Pick up the (*item*).	Y	N

Specific requests from your classroom:

20. *Please stop kicking the desk.*	(Y)	N
21. *Throw the spitwad away.*	(Y)	N
22. _____	Y	N
23. _____	Y	N

At least ten different requests marked across a week are required to use the formula below:

$$\frac{\text{Total "Y" Marks } \underline{6}}{(\text{Total "Y" Marks } \underline{6} + \text{Total "N" Marks } \underline{6})} \times 100 = \underline{50}\% \text{ Percent Compliant}$$

Adapted with permission from Jesse (1989).

© 2017 William R. Jenson

REPRODUCIBLE 3.1b

Guideline

In general, Electronic Home Notes with a target behavior of following directions is appropriate for students who comply at least 40% of the time but are below 80%—the compliance level for average students.

Definition

fol·low·ing di·rec·tions

The student follows a staff member's request within 3 to 5 seconds.

57

Steps for Completing the Compliance Probe

1. **Select at least ten and as many as 19–20 requests from the Compliance Probe Checklist.**

2. **Across a week, have the teacher make the requests.**

   The requests should be made naturally, using phrasing common to the teacher. No rewards should be offered for compliance, and no scolding or lectures should be delivered for noncompliance.

3. **Have the teacher record responses.**

   When a request is given, the teacher marks a "yes" if the student complies within 10 seconds. If the student does not comply with the request within 10 seconds, the teacher marks a "no." The teacher should not repeat the request during the 10-second interval. Other than making the initial request, the teacher should not coach the student to comply or otherwise interact with the student.

4. **Calculate the rate of compliance.**

   For the week, divide the total number of "yes" responses by the total number of requests. For example, 15 compliant responses divided by 20 requests = .75, or 75% .

Search and Replace

Identify Target Behaviors to Replace Misbehaviors

Objectively defined target behaviors are the core of well-designed Electronic Home Notes. This section provides guidelines for selecting goals that can help a student improve overall school performance. Target behaviors will be defined by the interventionist and teacher or the teacher-interventionist.

Objective

To effectively define target behaviors for an Electronic Home Note

"Look at me-e-e-e-e-e-e!"

Guidelines for Identifying Effective Target Behaviors

The final selection of target behaviors for the Electronic Home Note will be made by the student's teacher or in consultation with an interventionist. Five guidelines help define effective target behaviors.

- Select three to five target behaviors at any one time.

- Define observable and measurable target behaviors.

- Define positive target behaviors.

- Select central (keystone) target behaviors (defined in Box 3.2a on p. 63).

- Mix behavioral and academic target behaviors.

Guideline 1. Select four to five target behaviors for an Electronic Home Note program. As the student achieves success, target behaviors and goals can be changed to reflect current areas of need. Do not use more than five target behaviors at any one time.

Guideline 2. Define target behaviors objectively. Your goal is to leave little room for interpretation as to the meaning of the target behaviors. If you cannot see the behavior or measure it in some way, judging the occurrence of the behavior will be difficult and unreliable.

Definition

ob·jec·tive tar·get be·hav·iors

These behaviors are: 1) observable, 2) measurable, and 3) defined or stated positively.

An example of a too broadly defined target behavior is "be responsible." Although you may know what "responsible" behavior means, other people may have a different interpretation—especially the student. Common but broad target behaviors need to be broken down into their observable components. Table 3.2a below gives examples of overly broad target behaviors and positive examples of specific target behaviors.

Table 3.2a • Broad vs. Specific Target Behaviors

Overly Broad	Specific
Be responsible.	Be on time to class. Bring your materials to class. Work consistently across a work period. Follow directions right away.
Be respectful.	Let others talk. Use kind words and actions. (Avoid name calling, teasing, and put-downs.)
Be safe.	Walk. Keep your hands, feet, and other objects to yourself. Follow directions.
Show a positive attitude.	Make positive comments.
Be motivated.	Begin work right away. Turn your work in on time. Do your personal best.

Guideline 3. Define target behaviors positively. Ideally, target behaviors focus on increasing appropriate behaviors instead of decreasing inappropriate behaviors. A positively defined target behavior teaches the student what he or she should be doing versus simply telling the student to stop engaging in an undesired behavior. Positively defined target behaviors make Electronic Home Notes an overall positive experience. On the other hand, negatively defined target behaviors can make the Electronic Home Note program a demeaning experience for students and their parents. Table 3.2b on the next page compares negatively stated target behaviors and positively stated target behaviors.

Table 3.2b • Negative vs. Positive Statements of Target Behaviors

Negatively Stated	Positively Stated
Don't talk out.	Raise your hand and wait to be called on before speaking.
Stop being off task.	Watch the speaker during whole group instruction. Keep "quiet hands" during whole group instruction. Work independently on written work for 10 minutes with no interruption.
Stop hitting other students.	Keep your hands, feet, and other objects to yourself.

Guideline 4. Select keystone target behaviors and two or three behaviors that address specific problem behaviors. Even when target behaviors are defined objectively and positively, all target behaviors are not created equal. Changing some behaviors can actually affect and improve other related behaviors—making the behavioral change hugely beneficial. These influencing behaviors are called keystone behaviors (see Box 3.2a).

Pop-Up Box

Research

Electronic Home Notes has been shown to effectively improve a student's on-task behavior in the classroom, with a bonus reduction in problematic behaviors (Knorr, 2015; Lopach, 2016).

- **On task:** Staying on task is a keystone behavior. The average student in a general education classroom is on task approximately 85% of the time. Students who are chronically off task remain on task only about 50% of the time (Rhode et al., 2010). Improving the on-task behavior of students from 50% to 85% with Electronic Home Notes will effect an overall improvement in learning. **NOTE:** A 35% increase in on-task behavior amounts to about 10.5 hours per week for a 6-hour school day!

When keystone behaviors change, a frequent secondary effect also occurs. Problematic classroom behaviors such as talking out, out of seat, and bothering other students decrease automatically. The improved on-task behavior displaces other problem behaviors because the behaviors are incompatible. It is impossible to engage in the appropriate behavior and misbehavior at the same time.

- ***Following directions:*** Another example of a keystone behavior is following directions. Students who do not follow directions often demonstrate other interconnected behaviors such as arguing, being disrespectful, and breaking rules. Improving a student's compliance with following directions will result in a concurrent reduction in arguing, disrespect, and rule breaking.

By improving the keystone behaviors of being on task and following directions through a fully developed Electronic Home Note program, we often see a significant general improvement in a student's other disruptive behaviors as well as academic performance. Both "stay on task" and "follow directions" are excellent target behaviors for Electronic Home Notes because of their positive and broad influence over classroom behavior and academic performance.

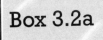

Box 3.2a

Keystone *Behaviors*

Each student is an individual with specific behavioral strengths and weaknesses. However, there are interconnecting behavioral patterns that students with behavior problems often demonstrate. The interconnecting problem behaviors act like stones in an arch. We like to call some behaviors *keystone* behaviors because they are like the keystone, or middle stone in an arch. Keystones hold an arch together. If you remove a keystone, the whole arch will fall apart. Problem behaviors are connected to keystone behaviors much like the stones in an arch. If you can reduce a problematic keystone behavior, related problem behaviors automatically improve.

In addition to "stay on task" and "follow directions," several other common behaviors frequently cause difficulties for students. Each of the behaviors below can be used alone or in combination with other target behaviors in the Electronic Home Note program. The following common target behaviors are observable, measurable, and positive.

- *Keep your hands, feet, and other objects to yourself (KYHFOOTY):* This is a good target behavior for students who consistently touch others, play with objects in the classroom, or are physically aggressive with others. It can be listed as KYHFOOTY.

- *Raise your hand before speaking:* One of the most distracting student behaviors in the classroom is talking out or speaking without permission. Talking out disturbs other students and interrupts the instructional flow. It is important to teach students an appropriate behavioral alternative such as raising your hand.

- *Use an appropriate voice level:* This skill may need to be explicitly taught to students because it requires that they know how to moderate their voice level according to the context. Different voice levels are appropriate for different settings (e.g. for outside, during group activities, in the hallway, and during independent work). Different teachers have different expectations, so it is important to clarify expectations.

- *Stay in your spot:* Students who are frequently out of their seats disrupt the entire class. For this target behavior, students need to be taught when and why it is appropriate to leave their seat and how to ask for permission if it's needed (e.g., for using the restroom, sharpening a pencil, or getting a drink of water).

- *Be prepared:* Students often do not have materials such as pencils, homework, textbooks, and writing paper. If "be prepared" is selected as a target behavior for Electronic Home Notes, a checklist should be made of all the materials the student needs in order to receive a positive home note rating.

- ***Keep cool:*** Keep cool is a good target behavior to include on Electronic Home Notes for students who are explosive or highly anxious, or have difficulty maintaining calm interactions with other students or adults (See Box 3.2b).

- ***Follow classroom rules:*** Following classroom rules can be an effective target behavior if the rules are explicit, easy to understand, and broken down into observable, measurable, and positive components. For some students, you may need to replace follow classroom rules with three more specific rules like: keep your hands and feet to yourself, follow directions right away, and stay in your seat.

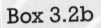

Box 3.2b

Teach Expectations:

Keep Cool

Some target behaviors require instruction. For example, the goal of keep cool, while observable and positive, requires that the student learn replacement behaviors. For keep cool, you can teach the following strategies:

1. Count to ten.
2. Tell yourself, "I can be cool."
3. Take several deep breaths.
4. Choose a way to be cool:

   - Tell someone how you feel.
   - Do something fun to feel better.
   - Ask to take a break.
   - Think about one of your favorite things.

Adapted from *Superheroes Social Skills* [multimedia program], by W. R. Jenson, J. Bowen, E. Clark, H. Block, T. Gabrielsen, J. Hood, K. Radley, & B. Springer, Eugene, OR: Pacific Northwest Publishing. Copyright 2011 W. R. Jenson, J. Bowen, and E. Clark. Used with permission.

Guideline 5. Include a mix of classroom behavior targets and academic targets. It is a good practice to mix classroom behaviors with academic skills. For example, you may want to include stay on task and follow directions with an academic target such as complete math problems during independent work or participate in reading group as defined by finger tracking, reading when asked, answering questions, and asking questions. Problem behaviors and poor academic performance are often linked and manifest concurrently in the classroom.

Box 3.2c

Positive Behavioral *Interventions and Supports*

Positive Behavioral Interventions and Supports (PBIS) programs have had a major positive effect on schools by significantly reducing discipline problems. The PBIS model consists of a three-tiered system of Tier 1 universal supports (all students), Tier 2 secondary interventions (some students), and Tier 3 targeted interventions (a few students). The Electronic Home Note program is highly effective when used in a school implementing a model of positive behavior supports.

Breaking down the most popular PBIS rules into more specific and understandable target behaviors makes the Electronic Home Note program far more effective when used with a school's PBIS system.

Three popular PBIS rules are be responsible, be respectful, and be safe. For most students, these global rules work. However, for many students who have behavior problems, these rules need to be broken down into observable behaviors. When general rules are broken down into observable behaviors for an Electronic Home Note program, students can learn to be responsible, respectful, and safe.

Tools for Identifying Target Behaviors

Identifying appropriate target behaviors for a student in a classroom is often easy to do because the student's inappropriate behaviors (or lack of appropriate behaviors) are overt. Sometimes a more systematic approach is needed when selecting target behaviors.

Importance of Classroom Behaviors Form

One approach is to learn about the teacher's expectations. The Importance of Classroom Behaviors form (Rhode et al. 2010) is a list of the 30 most common behavioral expectations of teachers. Have the teacher complete this form (Reproducible 3.2a) to identify the five top behavioral expectations if you need assistance in choosing target behaviors for a student. See Figure 3.2a on pages 68–69.

Behavior Checklists

You may wish to use a commercial behavior checklist such as the Behavior Assessment Scale for Children (Third ed; Reynolds & Kamphaus, 2015), the Child Behavior Checklist (Achenback & Rescorla, 2001), or the Conners Comprehensive Behavior Rating Scale 3rd Ed. (Conners, 2008). Each of these checklists consists of a series of questions relating to a student's behavior that a teacher rates on a Likert scale (e.g., 0=Never, 1=Sometimes, 2=Often, 3=Frequently). Review the teacher's ratings on the checklist and select the behaviors with the highest ratings to target with Electronic Home Notes.

Figure 3.2a • Importance of Classroom Behaviors

Electronic Home Notes

Importance of Classroom Behaviors (1 of 2)

Teacher: _____

Date: _____

Please rate how important it is to you that a student do the following:	Not important	Somewhat important	Moderately important	Quite important	Extremely important
I. Classroom Behavior					
The student:					
1. Listens quietly to directions	1	2	3	4	5
2. Follows oral directions accurately	1	2	3	4	5
3. Follows written directions accurately	1	2	3	4	5
4. Appears attentive during discussions	1	2	3	4	5
5. Is prepared with proper materials	1	2	3	4	5
6. Begins assignments promptly	1	2	3	4	5
7. Works quietly on assignments	1	2	3	4	5
8. Asks for help when needed, but not to excess	1	2	3	4	5
9. Turns in assignments on time	1	2	3	4	5
10. Follows classroom rules	1	2	3	4	5
11. Completes assigned tasks	1	2	3	4	5
II. Basic Interaction Skills					
The student:					
12. Contributes appropriately to discussions	1	2	3	4	5
13. Responds to the teacher's praise and attention	1	2	3	4	5
14. Engages in conversations appropriately	1	2	3	4	5
15. Makes requests appropriately	1	2	3	4	5

© 2017 William R. Jenson

REPRODUCIBLE 3.2a

Figure 3.2a (continued)

Electronic Home Notes

Importance of Classroom Behaviors (2 of 2)

Please rate how important it is to you that a student do the following:	Not important	Somewhat important	Moderately important	Quite important	Extremely important
III. Getting Along Skills					
The student:					
16. Participates in group activities	1	2	3	4	5
17. Follows rules on the playground	1	2	3	4	5
18. Follows rules in hallways and bathrooms	1	2	3	4	5
19. Is positive and friendly	1	2	3	4	5
20. Is cooperative	1	2	3	4	5
21. Gets the teacher's attention appropriately	1	2	3	4	5
22. Gets the attention of his or her peers appropriately	1	2	3	4	5
23. Gets along with others on the playground	1	2	3	4	5
IV. Coping Skills					
The student:					
24. Expresses anger appropriately	1	2	3	4	5
25. Uses appropriate language (no swearing)	1	2	3	4	5
26. Enjoys competition in the classroom or on the playground	1	2	3	4	5
27. Resists peer pressure	1	2	3	4	5
28. Disagrees appropriately	1	2	3	4	5
29. Accepts "No" for an answer	1	2	3	4	5
30. Accepts criticism or consequences appropriately	1	2	3	4	5

Once you complete the form, please place an asterisk (*) next to the five behaviors you consider most important for student success in your classroom.

© 2017 William R. Jenson

REPRODUCIBLE 3.2a

Cooper's Case Study, Target Behaviors

While meeting, Mr. James shares observation data for Cooper. The data match Ms. Anderson's perceptions. Ms. Anderson and Mr. James agree that On Task is the highest priority. This keystone behavior will positive affect Cooper's other target behaviors. Mr. James adds the target behaviors and descriptions to Cooper's Electronic Home Note.

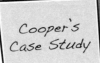

Cooper's Case Study

Proposed Target Behaviors

Consultation and Training Meeting: Ms. Anderson

Proposed Target Behaviors and Descriptions

1. On Task: Make eye contact with the teacher or task and perform only the requested task, math independent work.

2. Follow Directions: Follow a staff member's directions in 3 to 5 seconds.

3. Stay in Seat: Remain in seat. Leave only if requested or required (get materials, move to different activities at the right time).

4. Appropriate Voice Level: Use a voice level appropriate to the classroom activity.

Configuring the System
Set Up a Behavior Scale

Rating systems track student progress on each target behavior and provide all intervention participants with information on the student's performance. Each day, the target behaviors are rated by the classroom teacher and shared with parents via the Electronic Home Note. Ratings for the home note can be completed for a specific period of time (such as independent work for math or for a math period) or for a whole school day.

Objectives

- To select an effective rating system for the Electronic Home Note
- To determine reasonable goals with a 0–10 rating system
- To understand the Electronic Home Note rating system

Recommended Rating Scale

Research literature indicates that qualitative scales are more accurate and effective than quantitative scales (Box 3.3a). They also require less time and are more appealing to use. A scale of 0 to 10 has been shown (as reviewed by Chafouleas, Riley-Tillman, & Christ, 2009) to be an accurate assessment method for both academic engagement and target behaviors such as following directions and following classroom rules.

With Electronic Home Notes, we use a scale of 0 (Never) to 10 (Always).

Box 3.3a

Qualitative and Quantitative
Rating Systems

Two rating systems, qualitative and quantitative scales, have been identified in the literature to promote positive student functioning (Vannest,
et al., 2010).

Qualitative scales are retrospective (done at the end of a period of time)
and summative (provide an overall rating for a period of time). Common
scales range from 1 to 3, 1 to 5, or 1 to 10, with a rating of 0 representing
Never and the highest number representing Always.

0	1	2	3	4	5	6	7	8	9	10

Quantitative scales use frequency counts. For example, the observer
might make tally marks to track each occurrence of a behavior.

When to Rate Behaviors

The teacher's daily ratings can be based on the whole school day or selected periods such as independent math work.

Recommended Goals

We suggest starting with a goal of 7 or higher for most behavior targets. This corresponds to the behavior occurring approximately 70% of the time. For an on-task goal, the teacher's rating of 7 represents 70% of the time. **NOTE:** The rating is the teacher's best approximate assessment of the student's time on task and not an exact measure.

Increase Sophistication

Once a student has received a rating of 7 or more for 8 out of 10 days, the goal can be increased to 8 or higher for the target behavior. (For on-task behavior, this would translate to being on task about 80% of the time. Because the average student in a general education classroom is on task approximately 85% of the time, this target is approaching the norm.)

Components of an Effective Rating System

Once a plan is put together, it will include target behaviors, behaviors defined as observable goals, when the behaviors will be rated, the rating scale, and initial goals.

Table 3.3a on the next page provides examples.

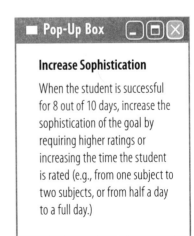

■ Pop-Up Box ⊟⊡⊠

Increase Sophistication

When the student is successful for 8 out of 10 days, increase the sophistication of the goal by requiring higher ratings or increasing the time the student is rated (e.g., from one subject to two subjects, or from half a day to a full day.)

Table 3.3a • Sample Target Behaviors, Time of Day, and Goal

Behavior	Defined as . . .	Time (by day, subject, etc.)	Rating Scale 0–10
Keystone: Stay On Task	Make eye contact with the teacher or task and perform the requested task.	Math instruction and independent work	Initial goal: 7 (increasing to 8)
Keystone: Follow Directions	Follow a staff member's request within 3 to 5 seconds.	All day	Initial goal: 7 (gradually increasing to 10)
KYHFOOTY	Keep your hands, feet, and other objects to yourself.	All day (or two half-day goals)	Initial goal: 8 (gradually increasing to 10)
Get Attention the Right Way	Raise your hand and wait to be called on.	All day (or two half-day goals)	Initial goal: 8 (gradually increasing to 10)
In Your Spot (Stay in Your Seat)	Stay in your seat, leave only when asked (e.g., lining up) or required (e.g., getting materials).	All day	Initial goal: 7 (gradually increasing to 10)
Be Prepared	Bring all materials on your checklist to class.	Beginning of the day	Initial goal:10
Use Appropriate Voice Levels	Use a voice level that is appropriate for the classroom activity.	All day	Initial goal: 7 (gradually increasing to 10)
Respect Others	Use compliments and nice words. Let others talk and listen.	All day	Initial goal: 7 (gradually increasing to 10)
Be Cool	Use the cool steps when frustrated.	All day (consider starting with 2 half-day goals)	Initial goal:10

Cooper's Case Study, Rating Scale and Goals

Ms. Anderson and Mr. James agree that a goal of 7 out of 10 (or 70%) is an appropriate goal for Cooper to start with. The goal is attainable but also represents improvement.

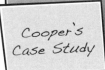

Cooper's
Case Study

Discussion of Rating Scale and Goals

Consultation and Training Meeting: Ms. Anderson

Proposed Target Behaviors

1. On Task: Make eye contact with the teacher or task and perform only the requested task.
   When: Math independent work   Goal: 7/10 (70%)

2. Follow Directions: Follow a staff member's directions in 3 to 5 seconds.
   When: Math independent work   Goal: 7/10 (70%)

3. Stay in Seat: Remain in seat. Leave only if requested or required (get materials).
   When: Math independent work   Goal: 7/10 (70%)

4. Appropriate Voice Level: Use a voice level appropriate to the classroom activity (same as others in class).
   When: Math independent work   Goal: 7/10 (70%)

Notes

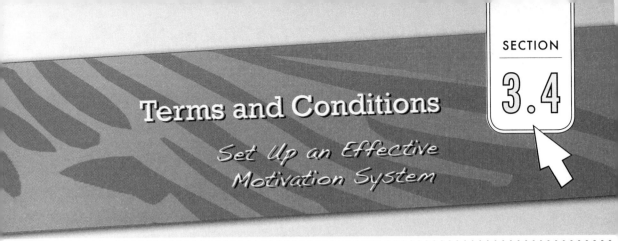

Terms and Conditions

Set Up an Effective Motivation System

This section will help you develop an effective reward system for Electronic Home Notes. A reward system is essential to an effective implementation.

Objectives

- To explain why some students need a reward system

- To identify the essentials of an effective reward system

- To determine how rewards can be earned

- To identify strategies for selecting rewards for a student

- To learn how to set up an effective reward system for Electronic Home Notes

The Importance of a Motivation System

Once you identity target behaviors and set up a rating scale, your next job is to set up a reward system. Though the majority of students seem to be naturally eager to behave in the classroom and meet academic requirements, about 3% to 7% of students need extra motivational support (Rhode, et al., 2010). No one knows exactly why some students need more motivational support. A combination of factors is likely to contribute, including a history of negative learning experiences, low academic skills, and family issues. Irrespective of the causes, home notes and associated reward systems have been shown by research to be one of the most effective ways of helping students who struggle to demonstrate positive outcomes in school (Atkeson & Forehand, 1979; Kelley, 1990; Vannest, et al., 2010).

Electronic Home Notes is designed to motivate students to succeed at school both behaviorally and academically. A well-designed Electronic Home Note program can help a student build up a reservoir of positive school experiences.

> *A well-designed Electronic Home Note program can help a student build up a reservoir of positive school experiences.*

Box 3.4a

An Analogy

Rhode et al. (2010) draw an analogy between people who suffer from heavy metal poisoning and students who are not motivated at school. People who suffer from heavy metal poisoning are slowly poisoned by what they eat. For example, some seafood can have small concentrations of arsenic and mercury. If you eat small amounts of these tainted foods over an extended period of time, the metals gradually build up in the body, poisoning you. Similarly, chronically unmotivated students may have been slowly poisoned by their own school failures and negative experiences over time. Most students can shrug off a few school failures; however, research shows that people tend to remember and perseverate on negative experiences more than positive ones (as reviewed by Tugend, 2012). Negative experiences and failures linger like heavy metals. Over time, negative school experiences may erode a student's motivation. These students may stop working, be reluctant to try new things, and misbehave in school.

Effective Rewards

A positive reward is anything that increases a behavior. It is not the "thing" the student earns but the increase in behavior that defines a positive reward or reinforcer. The exact "thing" may increase a behavior in one student (a positive reward) and decrease a behavior (punisher) in another student. For example, if a teacher yells at a student and the misbehavior actually increases, yelling is a positive reward. Similarly, if the teacher yells at a second student and the behavior decreases, yelling is a punisher. What defines yelling is how the student responds.

 Definitions

 **pos•i•tive re•ward**

A consequence that increases a behavior

pun•i•sher

A consequence that decreases a behavior

What Are the Features of an Effective Motivation System?

A reward's effectiveness is often determined by its system of delivery. A good reward system has the following essential characteristics:

- **Quick:** The system should not take a lot of time.
- **Simple:** The system should be uncomplicated.

■ **Pop-Up Box**

Variety Is the Spice of a Reward System

Unpredictable: A reward system that consistently motivates a student should occur at random and unpredictable intervals so the student is never quite sure if he or she will be rewarded or not. A common mistake is to deliver rewards on a fixed or known time schedule, such as every Friday or at the beginning of each day. Variability helps keep students behaving and working more consistently.

Anticipation Factor: Good reward systems include an element of surprise to build a student's sense of anticipation.

- **Inexpensive:** The system should not be too expensive to carry out.

- **Frequent:** The reward should be frequent enough to effectively change a behavior. The Electronic Home Note program suggests that a reward be given at least two to three times per week.

- **Immediate:** Earning and then receiving rewards should be immediate. Long delays between earning a reward and receiving it can reduce the reward's overall effectiveness.

- **Varied:** The reward system should be changed every so often. A sure way to reduce a reward system's effectiveness is to use the same rewards over and over again. It gets boring!

Effective reward systems are at the core of The Tough Kid series of behavior supports and are fully integrated into the Electronic Home Note program.

Earning Rewards With Electronic Home Notes

Select whether rewards will be given for reviewing the Home Note with the family or for a combination of reviewing the Home Note with the family and meeting a behavioral goal.

Single Reward

Research (Knorr, 2015) has shown that adding a reward that is contingent on the family's reviewing the Electronic Home Note with the student significantly improves students' classroom behavior and academic performance.

Dual Reward · Recommended

Research has shown that a dual-reward system significantly improves the target behavior and maintains consistent family review of the note (Lopach, 2016). With this option, the student is rewarded for:

1. Reviewing the Electronic Home Note with a family member, and

2. Meeting a target behavior goal

The student, the student's family, and the teacher must have an agreed-upon understanding of what constitutes meeting the goal Only one target behavior is rewarded at any one time.

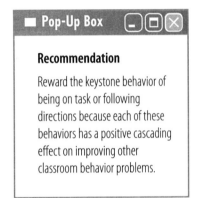

■ **Pop-Up Box**

Recommendation

Reward the keystone behavior of being on task or following directions because each of these behaviors has a positive cascading effect on improving other classroom behavior problems.

Steps in Setting Up a Reward System

To build an effective reward system, you will:

1. Identify six to 12 effective rewards.

2. Set up unpredictable Reward Days.

3. Select a system for delivering rewards.

STEP 1 • Identify six to twelve effective rewards.

We often fall into the trap of thinking we know what is reinforcing to a student. The cliché M&M is a perfect example. Are M&M's motivating? Yes and no. Some students like M&M's and some do not. Similarly, some students will be motivated by M&M's and some will not. Use the following procedures to help you create a list of rewards that will motivate the student you are working with.

1. **Ask the student.** Ask the student to tell you five to ten things he or she would really like to work for. These items can include:

   - Tangibles such as edible treats or small, age-appropriate items like pencils, erasers, or small toys

   - Activities such as games or being an office aide

   - Social interactions like a visit to the principal or a positive phone call home

2. **Use the Reinforcer Menu.** You may wish to use the Reinforcer Menu (Reproducible 3.4a) shown in Figure 3.4a to help the student select a reward or to create a list of rewards. This checklist is sometimes the most direct route to identifying effective rewards.

3. **Keep track of anything the student asks for frequently.** Ask the student's teacher or family what the student likes and frequently requests in the classroom or at home.

   NOTE: Students want what they ask for.

4. **Observe the student in the classroom or at recess.** Generally, students like what they do a lot in an unstructured setting. An activity they frequently engage in can be a natural reward.

5. **Use preference sampling.** Display an array of reward items or pictures of fun activities. Let the student name the items or activities he or she prefers.

Figure 3.4a • Reinforcer Menu

Electronic Home Notes

Reinforcer Menu

Student Name: _____

Instructions: Go over the list with the student and have the student check at least eight activities or items that sound good. If the student has other ideas, add them to the list.

1. Time to draw
2. Bring a friend for a treat
3. Computer time
4. Video game such as Guitar Hero, etc.
5. Messenger for the day
6. Extra recess or break time
7. Listen to a favorite song
8. Lunch with a favorite adult
9. Free time to read or be read to
10. Watch selected YouTube videos at lunch/break/recess
11. Homework coupon
12. Read announcements over the PA system
13. Popcorn treat
14. Juice
15. Free item from the school cafeteria
16. Choose a pen, pencil, or notepad
17. Coupon to school store
18. Discount coupon for a community business
19. Candy treat
20. Grab bag surprise
21. Temporary tattoo
22. Ice cream
23. _____
24. _____
25. _____
26. _____

© 2017 William R. Jenson

REPRODUCIBLE 3.4a

6. **Think like a kid.** Give up the idea of the classic but mundane M&M and think like a kid! Dollar stores, novelty shops, and flea markets are great resources for novel, inexpensive rewards. Students often like yucky things like edible boogers, terrible-tasting jelly beans, and objects that make weird sounds. Some students will even work for permission to break a rule—e.g., wear a hat or chew gum.

After deciding on a variety of rewards, write the items on a Reward Menu (Reproducible 3.4b). See Figure 3.4b below. We recommend making copies of the Reward Menu. Laminate the menus and use a dry-erase marker to list and frequently change rewards.

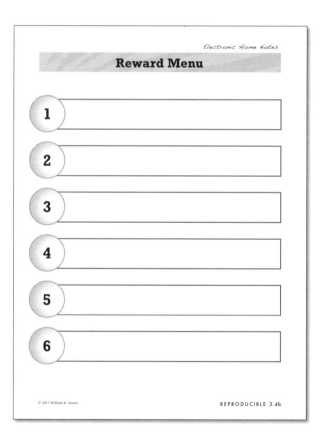

Figure 3.4b •
Reward Menu

STEP 2 • Schedule unpredictable reward days.

When the family reviews the daily Electronic Home Note with their child, they will send a reply via email to the interventionist. When you set up a Reward Day notice (using an out-of-office/vacation notice in Gmail), the family will receive a Reward Day notification (see Figure 3.4c).

Reward Days should occur on unpredictable days two to three times each week. This variability helps students work consistently to meet their goals.

Figure 3.4c • Sample Reward Day Notification Text

Congratulations! Your child has earned a Reward Day. Please tell your child to come to my office before school for a chance to win a prize.

Thank you for reviewing the Electronic Home Note with your child!

STEP 3 • Select a system for delivering rewards.

For the dual-reward system, the student earns a chance to win a reward on each Reward Day earned and a second chance to win a reward if the behavioral goal was met. In a single-reward system, the student earns a chance to win a reward for each Reward Day earned.

The following Tough Kid motivation systems have been shown to be highly effective.

- **Reward Spinner:** A reward spinner is made of a circle divided into six numbered wedges of varying sizes with a spinner in the center. The smaller wedges correspond to the more highly valued rewards on the Reward Menu. The odds of winning the high-value rewards are lower. For the dual-reward system, the student earns one spin and prize for each Reward Day earned by reviewing the Home Note with the family and one spin and prize if the target goal is met.

NOTE: You can build your own spinner using Reproducible 3.4c (shown in Figure 3.4d). Laminate the page onto poster board, cut on the dotted line to remove the arrow, and cut out the arrow. Fasten the arrow to the spinner's center with a small metal brad.

You can also find free electronic spinners with adjustable wedges online. Use the search term "adjustable spinner."

Figure 3.4d •
Reward Spinner

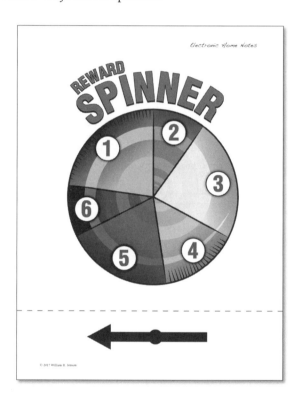

• **Mystery Motivator:** The Mystery Motivator (Figure 3.4e) is an envelope with a question mark drawn on it. The envelope contains a slip of paper that names a reward. The reward is a mystery. The Mystery Motivator should be something that is more highly valued by the student than the other rewards listed on the Reward Menu. When used in conjunction with the reward spinner, the Mystery Motivator is the smallest wedge on the reward spinner.

Figure 3.4e • Mystery Motivator

- **Throw a Die:** An alternative to the reward spinner is to have the student throw a die or dice. List six (or 12) rewards on the Reward Menu. The student receives the reward that corresponds to the number rolled.

- **Reward spinner and Chart Moves Board** (Reproducible 3.4d): Chart Moves adds another dimension of chance. The Chart Moves board (Figure 3.4f) includes 15 boxes. Boxes are bisected with diagonal lines—creating triangles. Using an invisible-ink pen, randomly place dots in the triangles (about one dot per three triangles). On Reward Days, the student colors half the box with a decoder pen for reviewing the Home Note and the other half for meeting a behavior target goal. If a reward dot appears in any triangle the student colors, the student spins the reward spinner for a prize. It's possible for the student to earn two spins of the reward spinner and two prizes, one spin and one prize, or no spins and no prizes.

Invisible-Ink Markers

Various types of invisible-ink markers are available. We recommend pens that have a writing tip and a decoding tip. You can search for "invisible ink pen" online or find instructions for making your own invisible ink.

Figure 3.4f • Chart Moves Board

Electronic Home Notes

Chart Moves Board *Version 1*

______________________'s Chart
(Student Name)

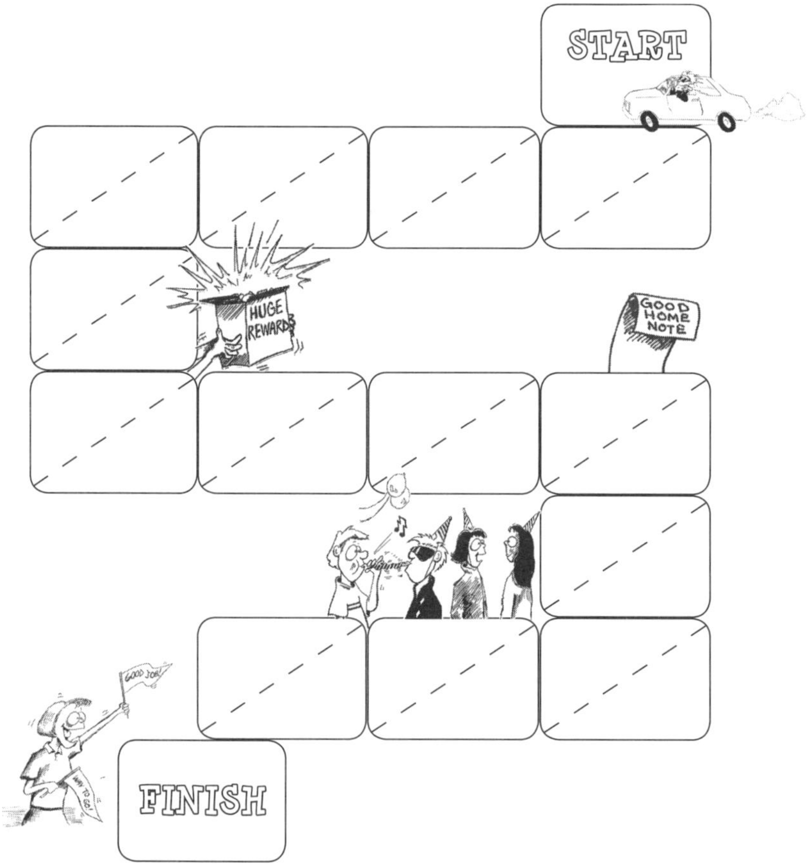
START
GOOD HOME NOTE
HUGE REWARDS
GOOD JOB!
FINISH

© 2017 William R. Jenson

REPRODUCIBLE 3.4d

- **Dot-to-Dot Reward Chart, Reward Spinner, and Reward Menu:**
  This reward system uses the computer dot-to-dot form (Reproducible
  3.4e), a spinner, and Reward Menu. See the dot-to-dot form in Figure
  3.4g on the next page. Each time the student earns an unpredictable
  Reward Day (by reviewing the Electronic Home Note with family), he
  or she gets to draw a line from one dot to the next. In addition, if the
  student met the behavioral goal on the day before the Reward day, he
  or she gets to draw another line from one dot to the next. (For example,
  if Wednesday is a Reward Day and the student reviewed his Home
  Note with his family and met his behavioral goal on Tuesday, the
  student gets to draw a line to two dots—one dot for reviewing the
  Home Note and one dot for meeting his goal.) When the student
  reaches a special reward dot, the student gets to spin the reward
  spinner and earns the associated reward from the Reward Menu.

Special Reward Dot Preparation

Option 1: To give the Dot-to-Dot Reward Chart the fun of random
rewards, use an invisible-ink marker to randomly color about one of
every three dots. Have the student use the decoder pen to connect the

Figure 3.4g • Dot-to-Dot Reward Chart

Electronic Home Notes

Dot-to-Dot Reward Chart

Student: _____

Start   Finish

© 2017 William R. Jenson

REPRODUCIBLE 3.4e

dots. When the student reaches the reward dot, the invisible ink will become visible.

Option 2: Randomly color in one of every three dots. Cover upcoming dots with a sticky note so the reward dots are not visible.

NOTE: To avoid a reinforcer slump, have some reward dots appear next to each other.

- **Reward Grab Bags:** Place 15 to 20 pictures of rewards in a paper bag. If the family has reviewed the Electronic Home Note and the student has met a behavioral goal, the student, without looking, draws a picture out of the bag and is rewarded with the prize shown. *Hint:* Place a Wild Card in the bag. If the wild card is drawn, the student chooses any reward.

- **Treasure Drawers:** This system requires a file cabinet with at least two drawers. The top drawer contains 10 to 15 rewards that are higher in value and the bottom drawer has 10 to 15 smaller reward items. A student who meets the target goal and reviews the home note with his family chooses a reward from the top drawer. A student who only reviews the home note with his or her family chooses a smaller reward from the bottom drawer.

Cooper's Case Study, Motivation System

Mr. James suggests the dual-reward system to reinforce reviewing the Electronic Home Note with a parent and meeting a priority goal. He also decides Cooper would enjoy the Chart Moves Board, online spinner, and Reward Menu.

Notes

Browsing the Files

Get Acquainted With Google Forms and Sheets

Y ou have explored important guidelines for identifying behavioral targets, selecting rewards, and setting up an unpredictable system for delivering the rewards. In this section, you will learn about the Electronic Home Note.

Objectives

- To understand the benefits of using Google to create an Electronic Home Note program

- To view examples of the Electronic Home Note components

- To see a practical application of the data collection for the Electronic Home Note program

- To see how Reward Days are triggered

- To explore confidentiality and FERPA issues as they apply to Electronic Home Notes

Benefits of Using Google

Google provides a variety of free online tools as well as online storage for your files. The Web-based applications you'll be using to set up Electronic Home Notes include Google Forms and Google Sheets.

With Google Forms:

- The teacher rates target behaviors each day

- Ratings are automatically sent via email to the family

The family and student review the Electronic Home Note and reply to the note via email. When an unpredictable Reward Day is scheduled, the family's reply triggers an automated Reward Day notification.

With Google Sheets, data are automatically:

- Stored in a spreadsheet for viewing at your convenience

- Displayed in a line graph for easy review and analysis

Sample Documents

This section shows samples of the files you will create using the Google platform. The directions for creating an Electronic Home Note include several detailed steps that are not difficult, but must be followed for easy success. Directions appear in a check-list format in Section 4.

The Google Form

The Electronic Home Note includes the student's target behaviors, the definition for each behavior, and a rating scale. *Optional:* The student can select a customized illustration or photo to create ownership in the Home Note. Check out Cooper's Electronic Home Note in File 6 on the next page.

The Home Note Sent Via Email

Once behaviors are rated by the teacher, the ratings are automatically sent via email to the family. See the sample in Cooper's Case Study box on the next page.

The Automated Reward Day Notification

The Reward Day notification is set up on unpredictable days by the inter-ventionist or teacher at the end of the school day. When the family replies to the emailed Electronic Home Note, an automated Reward Day notifi-cation is sent (similar to an out-of-office reply notice). See a sample in Cooper's Case Study box on the next page.

Cooper's Case Study, the Electronic Home Note

Mr. James is excited about the Electronic Home Note program. As an interventionist and former teacher, he has had great success with home notes, but a few failures due to the difficulty of keeping the home note going back and forth from school to home. Mr. James dives into creating the Electronic Home Note documents by carefully following the directions in Section 4.

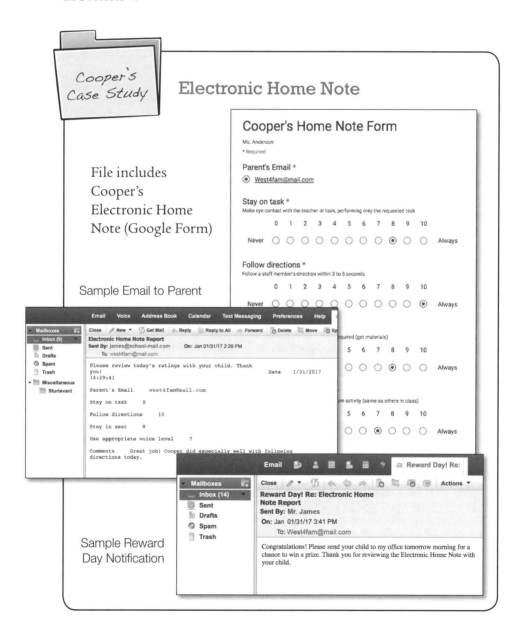

Cooper's Case Study

Electronic Home Note

File includes Cooper's Electronic Home Note (Google Form)

Cooper's Home Note Form

Ms. Anderson

* Required

Parent's Email *

⦿ West4fam@mail.com

Stay on task *

Make eye contact with the teacher or task, performing only the requested task

| 0 | 1 | 2 | 3 | 4 | 5 | 6 | 7 | 8 | 9 | 10 |

Never ○ ○ ○ ○ ○ ○ ○ ○ ⦿ ○ ○ Always

Follow directions *

Follow a staff member's direction within 3 to 5 seconds

| 0 | 1 | 2 | 3 | 4 | 5 | 6 | 7 | 8 | 9 | 10 |

Never ○ ○ ○ ○ ○ ○ ○ ○ ○ ○ ⦿ Always

Sample Email to Parent

Email   Voice   Address Book   Calendar   Text Messaging   Preferences   Help

Close | New ▾ | Get Mail | Reply | Reply to All | Forward | Delete | Move | Sp...

Electronic Home Note Report

Sent By: james@school-mail.com   On: Jan 01/31/17 2:29 PM

To: west4fam@mail.com

Please review today's ratings with your child. Thank you!   Date   1/31/2017
14:29:41

Parent's Email   west4fam@mail.com

Stay on task   8

Follow directions   10

Stay in seat   8

Use appropriate voice level   7

Comments   Great job! Cooper did especially well with following directions today.

...quired (get materials)

| 5 | 6 | 7 | 8 | 9 | 10 |

○ ○ ○ ⦿ ○ ○ Always

...m activity (same as others in class)

| 5 | 6 | 7 | 8 | 9 | 10 |

○ ○ ⦿ ○ ○ ○ Always

Sample Reward Day Notification

Email ▸ ▪ ▦ ▪ ▦ ⟲ | ✉ Reward Day! Re:

Close | ✎ ▾ | ↺ | ↞ ↶ ↠ | ▣ ▧ ▤ ▨ | Actions ▾

Reward Day! Re: Electronic Home Note Report

Sent By: Mr. James

On: Jan 01/31/17 3:41 PM

To: West4fam@mail.com

Congratulations! Please send your child to my office tomorrow morning for a chance to win a prize. Thank you for reviewing the Electronic Home Note with your child.

What Does the Data Management System Look Like?

Automated Collection of Behavioral Ratings in Google Sheets

The Electronic Home Note and a data collection spreadsheet in Google Sheets are linked. Data from the teacher's daily ratings and comments from the home note are automatically logged in a Google Sheet (spreadsheet) that can be accessed anytime to analyze behavioral trends. Check out Cooper's Google Sheet in the Case Study box on the next page.

Automated Line Graphs

A line graph can be automatically generated so data can be analyzed visually. See a sample graph in Cooper's Case Study box on the next page.

Cooper's Case Study, Electronic Home Note Data

As an interventionist, Mr. James knows how important data are in monitoring student progress, adjusting goals, and troubleshooting. (See Section 7 for more information on making data-based decisions.) He is looking forward to having a system that will automatically collect and graph data and that he can replicate for other students. See Cooper's Case Study box on the next page.

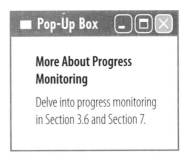

■ **Pop-Up Box**

More About Progress Monitoring

Delve into progress monitoring in Section 3.6 and Section 7.

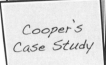

Cooper's
Case Study

Google Sheet (Spreadsheet for Data Collection)

File includes (at end of Intervention Week 1):

- Cooper's spreadsheet
- Sample graph

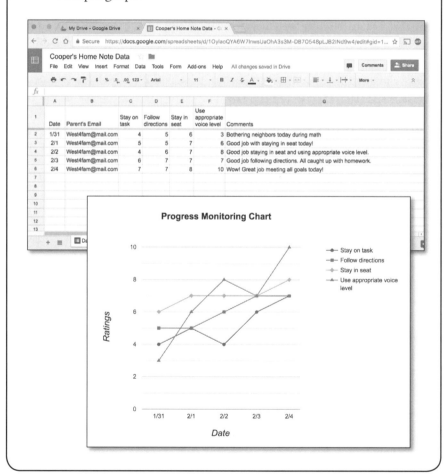

Confidentiality and FERPA Issues

When you use the Google platform, files are created and stored on the "cloud," Google's secure servers. Saving information on the cloud allows you to save, update, and access information through the Internet rather than storing it on a computer hard drive. Information stored on the cloud can be accessed from any electronic device (e.g., laptop, tablet, smartphone)—but only when you log into your Google account using the user name and password created when you set the system up.

The Family Educational Rights and Privacy Act (FERPA) requires schools to use reasonable methods to protect the confidentiality of student records. Schools should assess the security of information stored in the cloud and regularly update account security and other privacy settings. Because information is stored in the cloud, schools may wish to obtain written parent consent before implementing Electronic Home Notes.

Table 3.5a • FERPA and Confidentiality

Protected under FERPA: Information Requiring Consent for Disclosure	
Education Records	**Personally Identifiable Information**
Definition: Records that are directly related to a student and maintained by an educational agency or by a party acting for the agency	**Definition:** Direct and indirect identifiers
Examples • Performance ratings and grades • Health records • Student discipline files	Examples • Name • Names of family members • Addresses • Date of birth

Precautions

Follow all district guidelines regarding confidentiality.

Verify the family member's email address and double-check for accuracy when setting up the Electronic Home Note.

Ask teachers to be vigilant when they rate students. If more than one student is on an Electronic Home Note program, the teacher should always make sure to use the appropriate home note for a student's behavioral ratings.

NOTE: The only person who can access the collected data is the person who created the Electronic Home Note. While it may be beneficial to allow others to view the Google Sheets (e.g., teachers, parents, counselors, behavioral aides, and administrators), only the person who created the document can "share" access.

Taking a Screenshot
Progress Monitoring at a Glance

The Electronic Home Note program monitors student growth, includes tools for data-based decision-making with stakeholders, and assesses program satisfaction of the teacher, student and family. Information on how to use and interpret the tools and use data effectively is provided in Section 7.1.

Objectives

To preview use of the student's:

- Google Sheet and Chart

- Self-Plotting Graph

- Work samples

- Satisfaction feedback

To preview use of:

- Teacher and family feedback

- Follow-up observations in the classroom

CLASSROOM PROGRESS

Monitoring Student Progress and Satisfaction

On Reward Days, the interventionist or teacher-interventionist uses the following tools to monitor progress and satisfaction with the program.

Student's Spreadsheet

Because teacher ratings are automatically saved in the student's Google spreadsheet, the most current ratings and teacher comments are always available to review with the student and use for celebrations, adjusting goals, and troubleshooting. Charts can also be used to visually review trends in the student's data.

Student's Self-Plotting Graph

Self-Plotting is also included during the Reward Day meeting to encourage students to take ownership of their progress. On the Self Plotting Graph (Reproducible 3.6a), the student draws a goal line (e.g, 7 or 70%). Then, on each Reward Day, the student charts the teacher's ratings to create a visual reminder of successes and what he or she needs to do to reach the goal. See the sample graph in Figure 3.6a on the next page. (See Section 6.2 for additional examples with multiple goals.)

Student Work Samples

In addition to the student's daily ratings, work samples from the classroom are reviewed with the student on Reward Days. Work samples provide a way to monitor academic progress, reinforce the student for bringing materials, and look for opportunities to provide academic support and feedback as needed. For example, if the student has difficulty borrowing for subtraction, the interventionist can provide a quick tutorial

Figure 3.6a • Sample Self-Plotting Graph

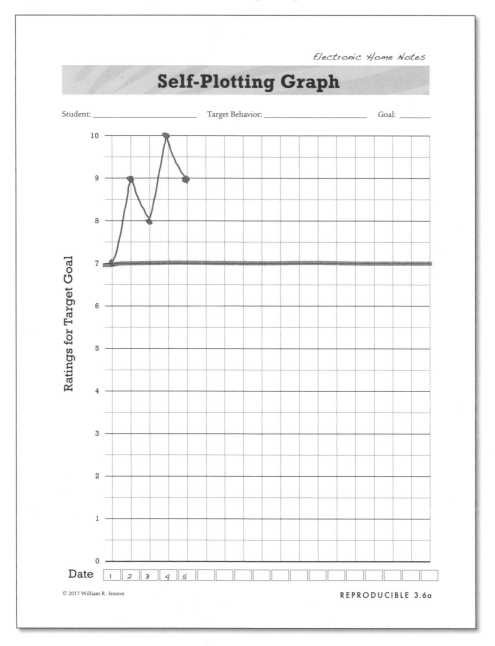

and share the deficit skill information with the teacher. When the student demonstrates the ability to borrow correctly, his or her progress can be acknowledged. (Additional information is provided in Section 6.3.)

The Student's Satisfaction Feedback

At least once a week, the student completes a Fun-O-Meter (Reproducible 3.6b) or Student Feedback Form (Reproducible 3.6c) and then discusses with the interventionist or teacher-interventionist what makes the program fun. Adjustments can then be made as appropriate. The student satisfaction tools provide tools for encouraging student ownership in the intervention process. See Figure 3.6b.

Figure 3.6b • Student Feedback Forms

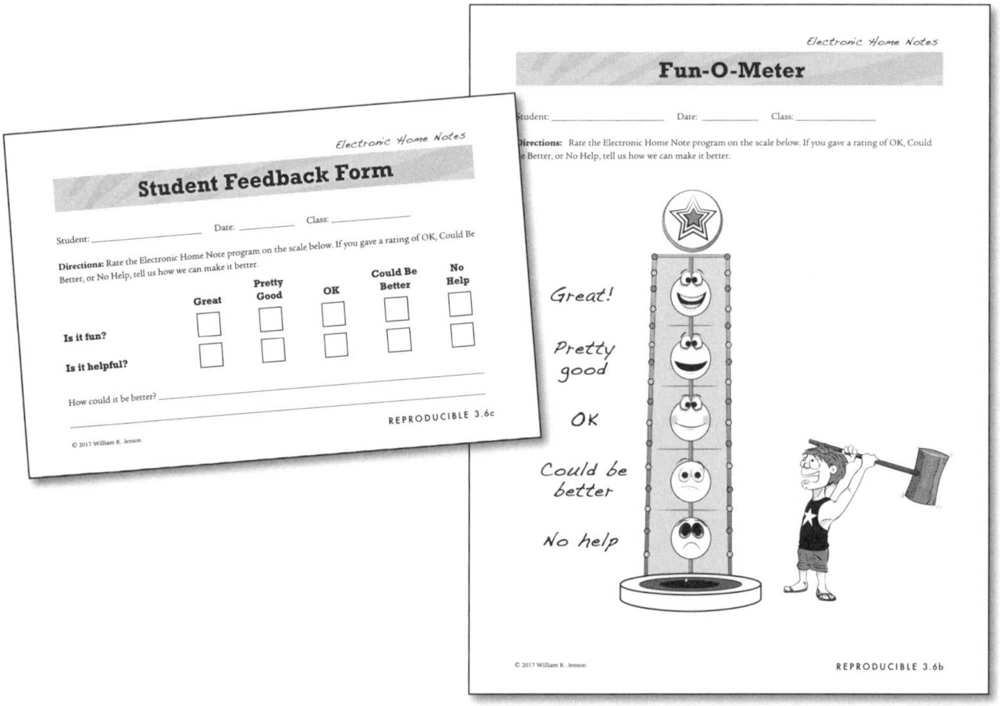

Monitoring Family and Teacher Satisfaction

The Electronic Home Note program includes options for monitoring teacher and parent satisfaction. The Family/Teacher Feedback Form (Reproducible 3.6d) can be sent via email or used during follow-up consultation meetings as a springboard for discussion. See Figure 3.6c on the next page.

Follow-Up Observations

Follow-up observations are recommended but optional. Use the Behavior Observation Form (Section 3.1) and/or the Follow-Up Observation Form (Section 5.5). Follow-up observations provide an opportunity to gather behavioral data in the classroom and compare pre-intervention data with in-program data. The observer's data can also be compared with teacher ratings to support ongoing reliability. Best practice suggests one observation per week.

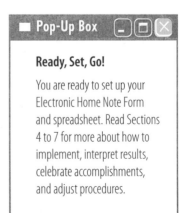

■ Pop-Up Box ⊟⊡☒

Ready, Set, Go!

You are ready to set up your Electronic Home Note Form and spreadsheet. Read Sections 4 to 7 for more about how to implement, interpret results, celebrate accomplishments, and adjust procedures.

Figure 3.6c • Family/Teacher Feedback Form

Electronic Home Notes

Family/Teacher Feedback Form

Teacher or Parent Name: _____   Date: _____

Student Name: _____

Directions: Circle 1–6 to indicate how well you agree or don't agree with Items 1–5. Use the scale below. For Items 6 and 7, please thoughtfully answer the questions.

Strongly disagree	Disagree	Slightly disagree	Slightly agree	Agree	Strongly agree
1	2	3	4	5	6

1. I like this intervention.   1   2   3   4   5   6

2. This intervention is effective.   1   2   3   4   5   6

3. I like the procedures and components used
    in this intervention.   1   2   3   4   5   6

4. I would suggest the use of this intervention
    to others.   1   2   3   4   5   6

5. This intervention did not have any negative
    side effects.   1   2   3   4   5   6

6. What aspects of this intervention do you like best?

7. What, if anything, would you change about this intervention?

© 2017 William R. Jenson

REPRODUCIBLE 3.6d

4.1 Home Note Users' Group

- Roles and Responsibilities for the Electronic Home Note Program
- Outline of the Electronic Setup Steps

4.2 How to Get Started With Google

- Google Chrome Browser
- Set Up a Dedicated Google Account

4.3 How to Create an Electronic Home Note

- Log In and Access Google Drive
- Create an Electronic Home Note Form
- Add Teacher and Parent Information
- Add Target Behaviors and Rating Scales
- Add a Comments Section
- When to Finalize the Home Note

4.4 How to Set Up a Spreadsheet and Automate the Email

- Set Up the Google Sheet
- Set Up Automated Emails
- Format the Spreadsheet

4.5a Next Steps for Teacher-Interventionists

- Set Up Notifications When Home Notes Are Sent (OPTIONAL)
- Fill Out and Send a Home Note

4.5b Next Steps for Interventionists

- Set Up Notifications When Home Notes Are Sent
- Give the Teacher Access to the Student's Electronic Home Note

4.6 How to Set Up Reward Day Notifications for the Student

Set Up Reward Day Notifications

4.7 How to Create a Chart in Google Sheets (OPTIONAL)

Create a Chart for Graphing Data

4.8 How to Share Data and Personalize the Electronic Home Note (OPTIONAL)

- Share the Data
- Personalize the Electronic Home Note Form

4.9 How to Organize Your Documents

- Create a Folder
- Move a File Into a Folder

Home Note Users' Group

Section 4 provides specific directions for setting up Electronic Home Notes using Google tools. Use the checklists provided in each step to avoid errors. See Box 4.1a on pages 113–114 for information about the online applications available with the Google platform.

Objectives

- To clarify the roles and responsibilities of interventionists when setting up Electronic Home Notes

- To clarify the roles and responsibilities of classroom teachers who are also serving as interventionists

- To preview the process of setting up an Electronic Home Note program

Roles and Responsibilities for the Electronic Home Note Program

Facilitated by a Teacher-Interventionist

When the Electronic Home Note program is initiated and run by a classroom teacher, the teacher plays a dual role. The teacher works with the family as an interventionist and sets up the program, creating the Electronic Home Note and data collection spreadsheet, sending out Reward Day notifications, and monitoring the student's progress. The teacher also serves in his or her regular role as classroom teacher by rating the student daily and sending the Electronic Home Note to the family each weekday evening.

Facilitated by an Interventionist

An interventionist works with a classroom teacher and family. The interventionist sets up the program. He or she creates the Electronic Home Note and data collection spreadsheet and works collaboratively with the classroom teacher and family to customize the home note form. The interventionist monitors that Electronic Home Notes have been sent and received, schedules and sets up Reward Day notifications, and monitors the spreadsheet and graphed data.

Outline of the Electronic Setup Steps

Sections 4.2 through 4.9 provide step-by-step checklists for how to set up the online components of an Electronic Home Note program. The task flowchart in Figure 4.1a on the next page shows the sequential steps to follow for either a teacher-interventionist or an interventionist. The amount of time required depends on your computer experience and how closely you follow directions. Once you learn how to set up an Electronic Home Note, it takes only minutes to set up additional students.

Figure 4.1a • Task Flowchart

Teacher-Interventionist	Interventionist
SECTION 4.2 Google Setup and Requirements	**SECTION 4.2** Google Setup and Requirements
SECTION 4.3 Create an Electronic Home Note: • Finalize With Family (Section 5.3)	**SECTION 4.3** Create an Electronic Home Note: • Finalize With Teacher (Section 5.2) • Finalize With Family (Section 5.3)
SECTION 4.4 Set Up a Spreadsheet in Google Sheets and Automate the Email	**SECTION 4.4** Set Up a Spreadsheet in Google Sheets and Automate the Email
SECTION 4.5A Next Steps for Teacher-Interventionists: Send the Electronic Home Note	**SECTION 4.5B** Next Steps for Interventionists: How to Get a Teacher Started
SECTION 4.6 Set Up Reward Day Notifications	**SECTION 4.6** Set Up Reward Day Notifications
SECTION 4.7 (OPTIONAL) Create Charts (late in the first week of implementation)	**SECTION 4.7 (OPTIONAL)** Create Charts (late in the first week of implementation)

111

Must-Dos

Read and check off each box. Setting up and running an Electronic Home Note program is easy if you follow directions carefully. (Also read the Do Nots. They are just as important as the Must-Dos.)

Follow directions.

Each direction is very important and has been tested and retested.

If you are unable to move forward in your setup, you may have skipped a step or executed an action out of order.

☐ I read this box.

Use the Google Chrome browser.

Google Chrome is the recommended browser.

To download, go to www.google.com/chrome/.

☐ I read this box.

Create a dedicated Google account.

Anyone who creates an Electronic Home Note must have a dedicated Google account.

See Section 4.2 for how to set up a Google account.

☐ I read this box.

Practice!

The first Electronic Home Note you set up will take some time and effort.

See Appendix A for how to set up practice files.

☐ I read this box.

Create a new name for new files.

For example, if you name a file Toby's Home Note and decide to delete it and start over, use a new name for the new file, such as:

- Toby M's Home Note
- Toby Madison's Home Note

☐ I read this box.

Ensure that the family member has email access.

The family member must have an email account that is easily accessible every weekday evening. Make sure you have the family's correct email address (review Confidentiality and FERPA Issues in Section 3.4).

☐ I read this box.

Do Nots!

Do NOT take shortcuts.

If you cannot move forward in your setup, you may have skipped a step or executed an action out of order.

☐ I read this box.

Do NOT copy or rename files.

Google security settings may prevent Electronic Home Notes created in this way from being sent.

☐ I read this box.

Do NOT use the same file name twice.

Do not simply delete a file and make a new home note with the same name. Google remembers and refers to earlier files even when they are in the Trash.

☐ I read this box.

Do NOT edit after linking the Google Form and Google Sheet.

Edits made after linking the home note form and spreadsheet may appear out of order on the spreadsheet or not show up at all.

☐ I read this box.

Box 4.1a

About the Google Platform *

Once you have set up your dedicated Google account, you will be using the following online tools for Electronic Home Notes:

- **Gmail:** Web-based email service. You will use Gmail to set up Reward Day notifications.

- **Google Drive:** Storage area for files you create using the free Google tools

*Also known as Google Apps or G Suite

(continued)

Box 4.1a (continued)

- **Google Forms:** An online application used to create forms to gather information and conduct surveys. You will use this tool to create the Electronic Home Note that the classroom teacher uses to review and comment on the student's behavior.

- **Google Sheets:** A spreadsheet application similar to Microsoft Excel. You will use this tool to store the data recorded in Electronic Home Notes and to automatically email the data to the family. Google Sheets also features tools you may use to create graphs showing student progress.

Updates and Troubleshooting

Google periodically updates the Google platform. Most changes will not affect your setup. If Google does change anything that affects setup, updated directions will be provided in the Reproducibles download (see Appendix C). Check the folder Google Updates. Google also provides support for the tools used in Home Notes as follows:

- **Google Drive:** https://support.google.com/drive

- **Google Forms and Sheets:** https://support.google.com/docs

- **Gmail:** https://support.google.com/mail

- **Google Accounts:** https://support.google.com/accounts

How to Get Started With Google

Your first step in creating an Electronic Home Note program is to create a dedicated Google account—that means this account will be for use with Electronic Home Notes only.

Objectives

- To install Google Chrome (web browser) if you don't have it already

- To set up a *dedicated* Google account to use for Electronic Home Notes only

- To learn how to log back into a Google account

Google Chrome Browser

Google Chrome is the preferred browser to use with Electronic Home Notes. It is a free web browser that can be used on Mac, PC, and Linux computers and Android and iOS phones. If you do not already have Google Chrome, go to www.google.com/chrome/browser to download and install the program. You may need to turn on cookies and JavaScript for the electronic components to work correctly.

■ Pop-Up Box

Browser Basics

We recommend you use the most current version of Chrome. However, Google tools should also work with the most recent version of:

- Firefox
- Windows only: Internet Explorer, Microsoft Edge
- Mac only: Safari

Set Up a Dedicated Google Account

You must have a dedicated Google account for your Electronic Home Notes.
If you don't, your Reward Day notifications will go to everyone who emails you. In other words, if you already have a Google account, *don't use it* for Electronic Home Notes.

- If you do not have an existing Google account, follow the directions in "Users Who Don't Have a Google Account" below.

- If you already have a Google account, follow the directions in "Users Who Already Have a Google Account" (starting on p. 118).

Users Who Don't Have a Google Account

____ 1. Go to **www.gmail.com**.

____ 2. Click the **Create account** link under the box. Ignore the **Enter your email** prompt.

____ 3. On the Create Your Google Account screen (see next page), enter your name, your desired username, a password, and the requested personal information. (The username and password allow Google to secure the confidentiality of your files.)

____ 4. Click on the blue **Next Step** button. (A Privacy and Terms box will pop up.)

____ 5. Read and scroll to the end, then click on **I agree**.

____ 6. A Welcome page will appear. Click on the blue **Continue to Gmail** button.

Google

Sign in to add another account

Enter your email

Next

Find my account

Create account ②

116

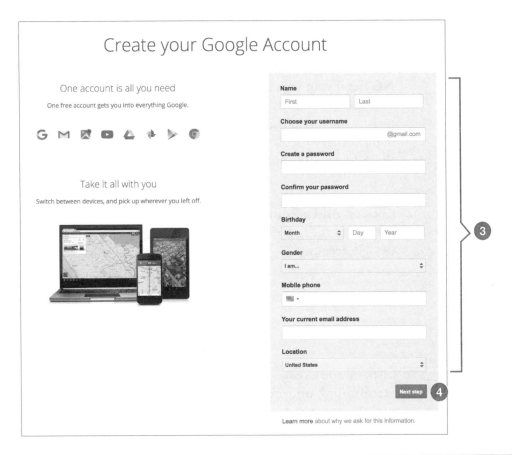

_____ 7. A new Gmail account Welcome screen will appear. Click the white **x** in the upper right-hand corner to close the screen. (A Take the Tour dialog box may pop up. If you haven't used Google before, you may wish to take the tour.)

Congratulations! Your new account is now set up.
Do not use this account for anything else.

NOTE: Ignore the **Setup Progress at 10%** message.

Users Who Already Have a Google Account

____ 1. Go to **www.gmail.com**.

NOTE: If your email account automatically opens, select your picture or icon in the upper right-hand corner of screen and then click the **Add account** button.

____ 2. Click on **Add account** at the bottom of the list of your existing Google account(s).

____ 3. Click on the **Create account** link under the box. (Ignore the prompt to Enter your email.)

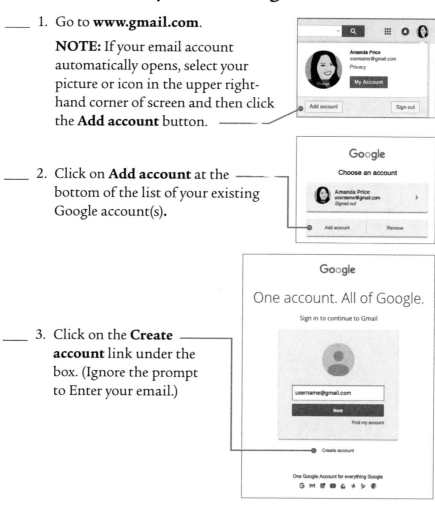

____ 4. On the Create Your Google Account screen (see next page), enter your name, your desired username, a password, and the requested personal information. (The username and password allow Google to secure the confidentiality of your files.)

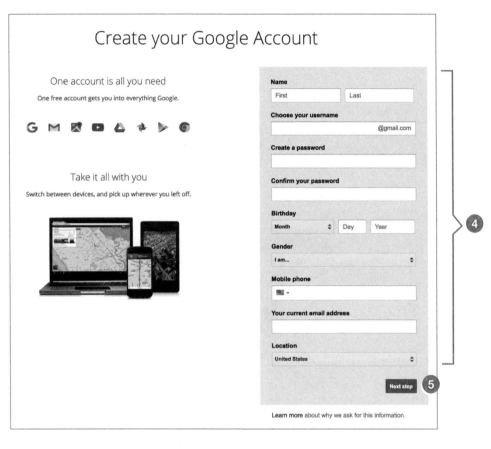

____ 5. Click on the blue **Next Step** button. (A Privacy and Terms box will pop up.)

____ 7. Read and scroll to the end, then click on **I agree**.

____ 8. A new Gmail account welcome screen may appear. If it does, click on the white **x** in the upper right-hand corner of the box to close the screen.

Congratulations! Your new account is now set up.
***Do not use** this account for anything else.*

119

Logging Back Into Your Account

Once you've set up your Google email account, log back in at any time from any computer.

____ 1. Open the Google Chrome browser and go to **www.gmail.com**.

____ 2. Choose your Electronic Home Notes Google account and sign in.

How to Create an Electronic Home Note

In this section, you will use the Google Forms app to set up your Electronic Home Note. Then you will tailor the form for a specific student. If possible, have the following information ready:

- The parent's email address

- Five or fewer target behaviors

- Descriptions of the target behaviors (what the behavior looks and/or sounds like)

Log In and Access Google Drive

____ 1. Log into your Google account (see instructions on p. 120).

____ 2. To access Google Drive, click on the **Google apps** icon ⠿ in the menu bar at the top right of the screen.

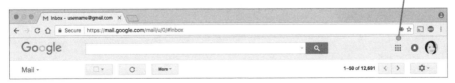

____ 3. When the pop-up menu appears, move your cursor over the **Google Drive** icon ▲ and click.

121

Create an Electronic Home Note Form

_____ 1. In Google Drive, click on the blue **New** button [NEW] at the upper left side of screen.

_____ 2. Place your cursor over **More** and select **Google Forms** from the menu that appears.

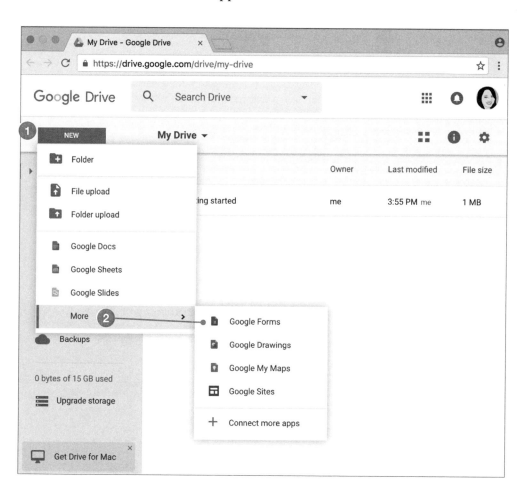

3. A blank, untitled form will be created. Name the form.

_____ 3a. Place your cursor over the text **Untitled form** in the upper left-hand corner.

_____ 3b. Click on the text and type "[*Student Name*]'s Home Note." **NOTE:** Whenever you are instructed to type text, type the text inside the quotation marks—do not include the quotation marks themselves.

_____ 3c. Then press the Tab key. Changes you make will be saved automatically, and the title on the form itself will also update automatically.

Cooper's Home Note

Add Teacher and Parent Information

____ 1. Place your cursor over the gray text **Form description** and type the teacher's name.

____ 2. Click on **Untitled Question**. Type the exact words "Parent's Email" and press the Tab key.

____ 3. Click on the gray pull-down menu at the right. Scroll down to **Multiple Choice** (if that selection is not already showing) and select it.

____ 4. Place your cursor over the text **Option 1**, then click and type the parent's email address. Press the Tab key. (If you don't have the email address, type "ENTER PARENT EMAIL" and replace with the correct email later.)

____ 5. Click on the **Required** slider (Required ⬤) to move the circle to the right to turn it on (i.e., to require a response).

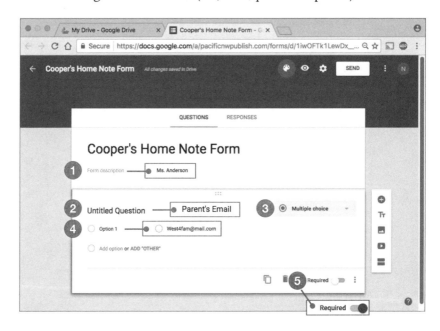

Add Target Behaviors and Rating Scales

1. Create Behavior 1.

    _____ 1a. Click on the **Add Question** icon ⊕ in the white bar next to or at bottom of the home note. (The box shown in Step 1b below will added.)

    _____ 1b. Click on the gray text **Question** and type the first proposed behavior goal (e.g., Stay on task).

2. Set up the rating scale of 0 to 10.

    _____ 2a. Select the gray pull-down menu to the right of the behavior goal you just entered. (**Multiple Choice** or **Checkboxes** may show by default.) Scroll down to **Linear Scale** ⟨⬩⬩⬩ Linear scale ▾⟩ and select it.

_____ 2b. Click the gray down arrow next to the first number beneath the behavior goal and select **0**.

_____ 2c. Select **10** for the second number.

_____ 2d. Click on **0 Label (optional)**, type "Never," and press the Tab key.

_____ 2e. Click on **10 Label (optional)**, type "Always," and press the Tab key.

_____ 2f. Click on the **Required** slider to turn it on (i.e., to require a response).

3. For each additional target behavior, repeat the following steps.

_____ 3a. Click on the **Duplicate** icon ⧉ to the left of the **Required** slider (see graphic above).

_____ 3b. In the duplicated behavior, type over the previous behavior with the next target behavior.

4. Add descriptions to each target behavior.

_____ 4a. Select the **Show** (⋮) icon (see graphic above) at the right of the **Required** slider and click on **Description**. (A new field with gray **Description** text will appear beneath the behavior field.)

_____ 4b. Click on the **Description** text and type the definition of the behavior you want to see (e.g., for On Task, "Make eye contact with the teacher or task and perform the requested task.").

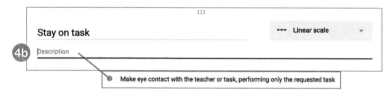

_____ 4c. Repeat steps 4a and 4b for each behavior.

When you have completed Steps 1–4, your form should look something like Figure 4.3a on page 129 (with one or more behaviors but no more than five behaviors).

NOTE: The Google Form (Electronic Home Note) must be edited and finalized with the teacher and family *before linking* to the Google Sheet (data collection spreadsheet), as described in Section 4.4.

How to . . .

DELETE A BEHAVIOR

Click on the behavior you wish to delete to make it active. (The active behavior has a thin blue line down the left side.)

Click on the **Delete** icon 🗑 to the left of the Required slider. For more on editing the Electronic Home Note Form, see Box 4.3a on page 130.

Add a Comments Section

The teacher can provide quick positive feedback to the family in the Comments (e.g., John is making a big effort to improve his behavior. I am proud of him! Thank you for your help.) The Comments section should appear at the end of the Electronic Home Note. See "Editing the Home Note Form" on page 130 for how to move form fields.

____ 1. Click the **Add Question** icon ⊕.

____ 2. Place your cursor on the gray **Question** text. Type "Comments."

____ 3. Select **Paragraph** from the pull-down list to the right of the field.

____ 4. Comments should be optional. Make sure the **Required** slider Required ⬭ is *not turned on* (i.e., the circle is to the left).

When to Finalize the Home Note

Teacher-Interventionists

Meet with the family to review the Electronic Home Note draft before finalizing it. Use the editing procedures in Box 4.3a to make any changes. See Section 5.3 for a family meeting agenda and training checklist.

Interventionists

Meet with the teacher and then the teacher and family together to review and finalize the Electronic Home Note. Use the editing procedures in Box 4.3a to make any changes. See Section 5.2 for a classroom teacher meeting agenda and training checklist and Section 5.3 for a family meeting agenda and training checklist.

Figure 4.3a • Electronic Home Note Form

Cooper's Home Note Form

Ms. Anderson

* Required

Parent's Email *

⊙ West4fam@mail.com

Stay on task *

Make eye contact with the teacher or task, performing only the requested task

	0	1	2	3	4	5	6	7	8	9	10	
Never	○	○	○	○	○	○	○	○	○	○	○	Always

Follow directions *

Follow a staff member's direction within 3 to 5 seconds

	0	1	2	3	4	5	6	7	8	9	10	
Never	○	○	○	○	○	○	○	○	○	○	○	Always

Stay in seat *

Remain in seat. Leave only if requested or required (get materials)

	0	1	2	3	4	5	6	7	8	9	10	
Never	○	○	○	○	○	○	○	○	○	○	○	Always

Use appropriate voice level *

Use a voice level appropriate to the classroom activity (same as others in class)

	0	1	2	3	4	5	6	7	8	9	10	
Never	○	○	○	○	○	○	○	○	○	○	○	Always

Comments

_____

[SUBMIT]

■ Pop-Up Box ⬁⬁⬁

No Need to Save!

With Google online tools (such as Forms, Sheets, and Docs), whenever you make any changes or close a file, it is automatically saved.

Box 4.3a

Editing the *Home Note Form*

To Delete a Behavior

- Click on the behavior you wish to delete.
- Click on the **Delete** icon 🗑 at bottom right.

To Add a Behavior

If you have already added a behavior, simply copy the behavior and revise:

- Click on the **Duplicate** icon ⧉ to the left of the **Required** slider.
- In the duplicate item, replace all fields with new information.

If no behaviors are currently defined in the Electronic Home Note, see "Add Target Behaviors and Rating Scales" starting on page 125.

To Revise a Behavior or Its Description

Click on the existing text and type over it.

To Change the Order of Items

- Click on the item you wish to move. A thin blue line on the left side indicates the field is active.
- Move your cursor over the six dots (⠿) at the top of the active box until the cursor changes to Move mode ✜ (four arrows).
- Click to select the box, then drag and drop it to the location (sequence) where you wish it to appear.

IMPORTANT: Once you set up the spreadsheet (Google Sheet) or start the Electronic Home Note program, any revisions to an Electronic Home Note require starting over by creating a new Electronic Home Note with a new name.

How to Set Up a Spreadsheet and Automate the Email

The next step is to link the Electronic Home Note to a spreadsheet in which the teacher's ratings and comments are stored. Within the spreadsheet, you will set up a script that automatically emails the student's ratings and teacher comments to the family whenever the teacher sends (submits) an Electronic Home Note.

NOTE: Make sure your home note is final before starting this step. When this step is complete, revisions made to the form won't automatically update the spreadsheet. If you need to make changes, create a new home note with a new name.

Objectives

- To set up a student's Electronic Home Note spreadsheet
- To automate the email home

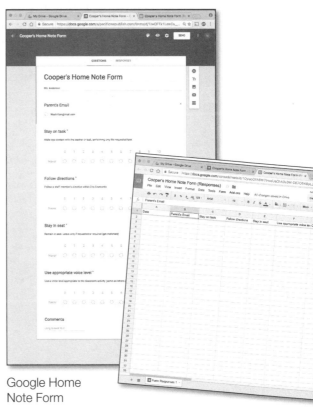

Google Home Note Form

Google Home Note Sheet

131

Set Up the Google Sheet

The Google Sheet is the spreadsheet that will store all of the teacher's home note data.

____ 1. In your Electronic Home Note, click on **RESPONSES** at the top right of the form.

____ 2. In the box that pops up, click on the green **Spreadsheet** icon ⊞ at the top right of box. (A Select Response Destination box will appear. By default, the **Create a new spreadsheet** option will be selected.)

____ 3. Click on **Create** at the bottom right of the box, and a blank spreadsheet will open (see graphic on next page).

This spreadsheet is linked to the Electronic Home Note Form you set up and will be automatically updated with information from all home notes completed by the teacher.

Set Up Automated Emails

In this step, you will enter a simple program (a script) that contains a series of commands. The script is triggered when the teacher enters daily behavioral ratings and clicks the Submit button on the Electronic Home Note. When the code is triggered, an email will be automatically sent to the parent.

133

1. Set up the script that automates the sending of daily Electronic Home Note data to the family.

_____ 1a. Copy the Code.txt file from the Electronic Home Notes download folder to your desktop, then open the file.

_____ 1b. Copy the contents.

_____ 1c. Click on **Tools** in the menu bar at the top of the spreadsheet and select **Script editor** from the pull-down menu.

_____ 1d. Select any code that already appears in the script editor window and paste the new code over it.

_____ 1e. Click on the **Save** icon 💾 in the menu bar. (The Edit Project Name box will appear.)

_____ 1f. Type "Code" in the highlighted **Untitled project** field, and then click on the **OK** button.

2. Set up a trigger to run the script you just created.

_____ 2a. With the script editor still open, click on **Resources** in the menu bar at top and select **Current project's triggers** from the pull-down list.

_____ 2b. Click on **No triggers set up. Click here to add one now**.

_____ 2c. Change **Time-driven** in the pull-down list to **From spreadsheet**.

_____ 2d. Change **On open** in the pull-down list to **On form submit**.

_____ 2e. Click on the **Save** button. (An Authorization Required box will appear.)

_____ 2f. Click on the **Review Permissions** button, then the blue **Allow** button in the next pop-up box.

_____ 2g.   Close the script editor tab by clicking the **x** on the browser tab at the top of your screen. If the spreadsheet does not become the active tab in your browser, select the tab with the spreadsheet icon and the name of your spreadsheet.

Box 4.4a

Advanced Tip: _Editing the Parent's Email Message_

The family note currently says, "Please review today's ratings with your child. Thank you!" If you wish to revise the note:

1. Click on **Responses** at the top right of the Home Note.

2. Click the green **Spreadsheet** icon at the top right of box.

3. Click **Tools** in the menu bar at the top of the spreadsheet and select **Script editor** from the pull-down menu.

In the code, the note to the family is inside the quotation marks. You can edit the text inside the quotation marks, but **DO NOT** change any other part of the code. (Even spaces affect how the code works.)

 5. Click the **Save** icon in the menu bar.

Bonus Tip: If you change the script and it no longer works, return to the original Code.txt file, copy its contents, and paste them into the script editor to replace the broken script.

Format the Spreadsheet

____ 1. With the spreadsheet open, place your cursor next to **A** above the **Timestamp** column head and click to select the entire column. (The column will be highlighted if it's selected.)

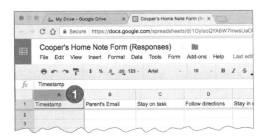

____ 2. Select **Format** in the menu bar and scroll down to **Number**. Move your cursor over **More Formats**, and finally **More date and time formats...** and click.

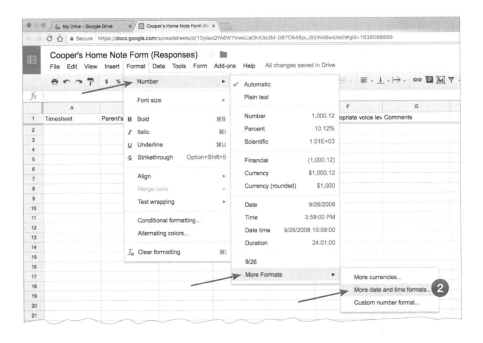

____ 3. Select the format that shows the month and day only—displayed as numbers, not text (e.g., "9/26")—and click on the blue **Apply** button.

____ 4. Double-click on the text **Timestamp** in Column A and replace with "Date."

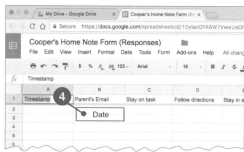

NOTE: In Section 4.7, you will learn how to create graphs from the spreadsheet so you can visually track data trends. This is easier to do once the teacher has recorded some data, so this step will be completed at the end of Week One.

You should now have two files created in your Google Drive for Electronic Home Notes—a home note form and a spreadsheet.

GOOGLE TIP: Your files may appear in a grid view. To view your files as a list, click on the **List View** icon ☰ at the top right of the Google Drive menu bar.

STOP!

Teacher-interventionists proceed to Section 4.5a.
Interventionists proceed to Section 4.5b.

Next Steps for Teacher-Interventionists

This section provides teacher-interventionists with the steps for filling out an Electronic Home Note. When you complete the steps in this section, skip Section 4.5b and proceed to Sections 4.6–4.7 to learn how to set up Reward Day notifications and chart student progress.

INTERVENTIONISTS

Proceed to Section 4.5b on page 143. Teacher-interventionists, continue reading.

Objectives

To learn how to:

- Receive an email notification that the Electronic Home Note went out
- Fill out and send the Electronic Home Note

Set Up Notifications When Home Notes Are Sent (OPTIONAL)

Follow these steps to receive an email notification that the Electronic Home Note has been sent. The email notification will let you know that the system is working.

If you elect to skip this option, close all browser tabs (click on **x** in each tab).

_____ 1. Click on **Tools** in the menu bar and select **Notification rules...** (A Set Notification Rules box will pop up.)

_____ 2. Select the bubble next to **A user submits a form**.

_____ 3. Select the bubble next to **Email – right away**.

_____ 4. Click on the **Save** button.

_____ 5. Click on the **Done** button in the next pop-up box.

_____ 6. Close all browser tabs (click on **x** in each tab).

Fill Out and Send a Home Note

____ 1. From Google Drive in your dedicated Electronic Home Notes account, open the student's Home Note by double-clicking on the file.

____ 2. From the menu bar at the top of the screen, select the **Preview** icon . (This will open the form so you can input information.)

____ 3. Enter ratings and comments (see graphic on next page).

____ 4. Press the **Submit** button (see graphic on next page). An email with the ratings and any comments will automatically be sent to the family.

Figure 4.5a on the next page shows a sample completed Electronic Home Note Form and email to parents.

Figure 4.5a • Sample Electronic Home Note Form and Parent Email

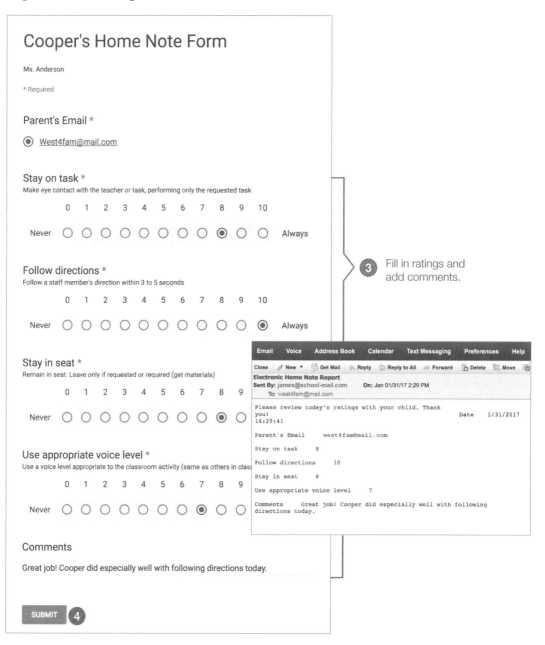

Next Steps for Interventionists

This section provides interventionists with directions for setting up the classroom teacher to access and use Electronic Home Notes. When you complete these steps, continue to Sections 4.6–4.7 to learn how to set up Reward Day notifications and charting.

> **TEACHER-INTERVENTIONISTS**
>
> Skip this section. Proceed to Section 4.6 on page 147.

Objectives

To learn how to:

- Receive email notifications when Electronic Home Notes are sent to the family

- Give the classroom teacher access to a student's Electronic Home Note Form

- Teach the teacher how to complete and send an Electronic Home Note

Set Up Notifications When Home Notes Are Sent

Follow these steps to receive an email notification whenever a teacher completes an Electronic Home Note and ratings are sent to the family.

____ 1. Click on **Tools** in the menu bar and select **Notification rules...** (A Set Notification Rules box will pop up.)

____ 2. Select the bubble next to **A user submits a form**.

____ 3. Select the bubble next to **Email – right away**.

____ 4. Click on the **Save** button.

____ 5. Click on the **Done** button in the next pop-up box.

____ 6. Close all browser tabs (click on **x** in each tab).

Give the Teacher Access to the Student's Electronic Home Note

Before providing access to the Electronic Home Note, ensure the teacher has the "How to Fill Out and Send Home Note" handout (Reproducible 4.5b) shown in Figure 4.5a on the next page.

_____ 1. From your Google Drive Electronic Home Note main menu, double-click on the Google Form to open it.

_____ 2. Click the **Send** button at the top right of the screen. (A Send Form box will pop up—see graphic below right.)

_____ 3. Input the teacher's email address in the **To** field.

_____ 4. Type "Home Note" in the **Subject** field.

_____ 5. In the **Message** field, type something like "Hi, Annie, Attached is the form we discussed during our meeting. Use the directions I shared with you to put the link to the home note on your desktop."

   IMPORTANT: *Do not check* the **Include form in email** box.

_____ 6. Click on **Send** at the bottom right of the window. (**NOTE:** Sending the Electronic Home Note form allows the teacher to fill out the form but not edit it.)

Figure 4.5b • Handout for Classroom Teacher

Electronic Home Notes

How to Fill Out and Send Home Note

GETTING READY

☐ 1. Open the email that the interventionist sent with the link to the Electronic Home Note.

☐ 2. Click on the **Fill Out Form** button. This will open the Electronic Home Note in Google Apps. **NOTE:** The form will open in your default browser (e.g., Chrome, Safari, Firefox, etc.).

☐ 3. With the Electronic Home Note open, click on the URL in your web browser address bar (or lock icon 🔒 if there is one) and drag it to your desktop. See "Browser Basics" below.

URL

My Drive - Google Drive | Cooper's Home Note Form - | Cooper's Home Note Form (R
🔒 Secure   https://**docs.google.com**/a/pacificnwpublish.com/forms/d/1iwOFTk1LewDx__5EgRT3Wf0FTHOA-3of6Of4tXeasQY/edit

← Cooper's Home Note Form   All changes saved in Drive

☐ 4. Close your browser and quit your browser application. Then check that the link works— re-open the Electronic Home Note by double-clicking on the icon on your desktop.

COMPLETING AND SENDING A HOME NOTE TO THE FAMILY

1. Fill out the student ratings and comments, and send the email to the family.

☐ 1a. Double-click on the Electronic Home Note icon on your desktop.

☐ 1b. Click on the bubble for the Parent Email address (select only one address).

☐ 1c. Complete all the behavior ratings by selecting the appropriate numbers.

☐ 1d. Add comments.

2. Send the Home Note.

☐ Click on **Submit**. (Data will be automatically emailed to the parent when you click **Submit**.)

NOTE: You can practice filling in the bubbles, etc., but DO NOT click on **Submit** until you are ready to send an Electronic Home Note to the family.

Browser Basics

According to Google, Google Apps work with the two most recent versions of these browsers:

- Chrome
- Firefox
- Windows only: Internet Explorer, Microsoft Edge
- Mac only: Safari

Other browsers may work, but you may not be able to use all features. For best results, make sure you are using an up-to-date version of a supported browser. Also make sure cookies and JavaScript are turned on for the browser. You can download the latest version of the Google Chrome browser here: www.google.com/chrome/browser/desktop/.

© 2017 William R. Jenson

How to Set Up Reward Day Notifications for the Student

Reward Day notifications are set up on the first day an Electronic Home Note program is used with one or more students. **NOTE:** There are several options to consider when designing your motivation system. Make sure you read Section 3.4 in the book.

Reward Day notifications from a single interventionist or teacher-interventionist cannot be tailored to individual students. They are global notifications—meaning that all students and families who receive daily ratings from your Google account dedicated to Electronic Home Notes will get the same message and be notified on the same day.

Set Up Reward Day Notifications

_____ 1. From your Electronic Home Notes Google Drive, click on the **Google apps** icon ⦂⦂⦂ (at top right) and select the **Mail** icon to open Gmail.

_____ 2. Click on the **Settings** button on the top right of the screen, then scroll to and select **Settings** from the pull-down list.

147

____ 3. In the **General** tab, scroll down to **Vacation responder** and select the bubble next to **Vacation responder on**.

____ 4. Input the date that you want the Reward Day notifications sent in the **First day** field. Leave the **Last day** box unchecked.

____ 5. Type "Reward Day!" in the **Subject** field and a note in the message box, such as:

Example 1: All students on home notes will report in at the same time.

Congratulations! Please send your child to my office tomorrow morning for a chance to win a prize. Thank you for reviewing the Electronic Home Note with your child!

Example 2: Smaller groups of students on home notes will report at different times.

Congratulations! Please send your child to my office for a chance to win a prize. Thank you for reviewing the Electronic Home Note with your child. We appreciate your participation.

- *First and second grade: Report in at morning recess.*
- *Third through fifth grade: Report in before school.*

____ 6. Click on **Save Changes** at the bottom of the window.

Important Routines for Reward Days

Turn on the Reward Day notification (Vacation Responder) before students go home the day before a Reward Day. If a Reward Day is scheduled, the Vacation Responder needs to be on before the family reviews the Home Note.

Turn off the Responder before the first morning recess or break on the day of the reward.

Make sure the family has the Family's Checklist (Reproducible 5.3b) so they know what to do when they receive a Reward Day notification. (See Section 5.3.)

■ **Pop-Up Box** ⊟ ▢ ⊠

Reward Day Notification

The Vacation Responder sends an Out-of-Office reply to anyone who emails you at your dedicated Electronic Home Notes email address. **Do not** use your dedicated Gmail account for any other correspondence.

What's Happening Behind the Scenes

When a parent (or family member) replies to an Electronic Home Note, the interventionist or teacher-interventionist receives an email from the parent. The parent's reply goes to the Gmail address you created when you signed up for the dedicated Google account. When the Reward Day notification (Vacation Responder) is on, the parent receives an automatic Reward Day notification in response to the reply email he or she sent. The next day, the student will follow procedures to participate in the reward system (e.g., report to the interventionist or meet with the teacher).

Notes

How to Create a Chart in Google Sheets (OPTIONAL)

A t the end of the first week, you may wish to set up the automated charting of each student's data. Charts should be set up after some data have been collected.

Objective

To use Google Sheet tools to create a chart to display Electronic Home Note data

Create a Chart for Graphing Data

See Section 7.1 for more information about graphing and the benefits of using Google Sheet charts to analyze data.

_____ 1. In Google Drive, open the spreadsheet associated with the student's Electronic Home Note.

_____ 2. Click on **Insert** in the menu bar and select **Chart**. (This will open the Chart Editor window.)

____ 3. Click on the **Chart types** tab (if it's not already active).

> **Chart Editor**
>
> Recommendations | **Chart types** | Customization ③
>
> 'Form Responses 1'!A1:A1003, 'Form Responses 1' ⊞ 4a

____ 4. Set the data range.

____ 4a. Click the small **Select data range** icon ⊞ directly beneath the **Chart types** tab label.

____ 4b. When the What data? box pops up, select column A in the spreadsheet by clicking on the letter **A** at the top of the first column.

> 4b
>
> **What data?**
>
> 'Form Responses 1'!A:A
>
> 4c Add another range
>
> OK   Cancel

____ 4c. Next, click on the **Add another range** link in the What data? box.

____ 4d. Select all columns with behavioral ratings data. (**NOTE:** Do not select the Comments column.) For example, if the student is working on five behaviors, select columns C–G. To select multiple columns, click on the letter at the top of the first column, hold down the Shift key, and click on the letter at the top of the last column. Selected columns will be highlighted.

> **What data?**
>
> 'Form Responses 1'!A:A   x
>
> 'Form Responses 1'!C:F   4d   x
>
> Add another range
>
> 4e OK   Cancel

____ 4e. Click on the blue **OK** button.

____ 4f. Select **Combine ranges: Horizontally** beneath the data range (see graphic on next page).

5. Set the data labels, and select the type of chart.

_____ 5a. Check the **Use row 1 as headers** box.

_____ 5b. Check the **Use column A as labels** box.

_____ 5c. Select the first **Line** chart icon ⌧.

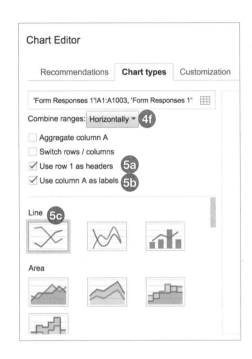

6. Name the chart.

_____ 6a. Click on the **Customization** tab.

_____ 6b. Replace **Chart title** With "Progress Monitoring Chart."

7. Set the x- and y-axis labels.

_____ 7a. Using the scroll bar, scroll down to **Axis**. Select **Horizontal** from the pull-down list.

_____ 7b. Type "Date" in place of **Horizontal axis title**.

_____ 7c. Next, select **Left Vertical** from the pull-down menu next to **Axis**.

_____ 7d. Type "Ratings" in place of **Left vertical axis title**.

_____ 7e. Scroll down further (if needed) to the **Min** and **Max** fields. Type "0" and "10" in the boxes, respectively.

_____ 7f. Click on the blue **Insert** button. A chart with a week's worth of data will open. (See the chart on the next page.)

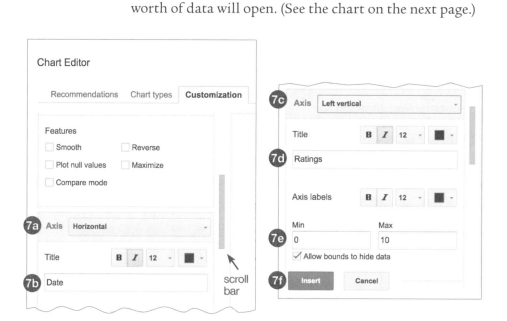

NOTE: There are many ways to customize your chart beyond what is explained here. Feel free to explore the other items in the **Customization** tab to make your chart as visually pleasing as possible.

8. Move the chart to its own page in the spreadsheet.

____ 8a. Select the chart by clicking on it if it's not already selected (framed with blue lines and squares).

____ 8b. Click on the small gray down arrow at top right of chart, scroll to **Move to own sheet...**, and click. This will create a new sheet in the file with the chart only.

____ 8c. Rename the sheet with the chart. Double-click on the **Chart1** text in the tab at the bottom of sheet, type "Home Note Chart," and press the Return key (see graphic on next page).

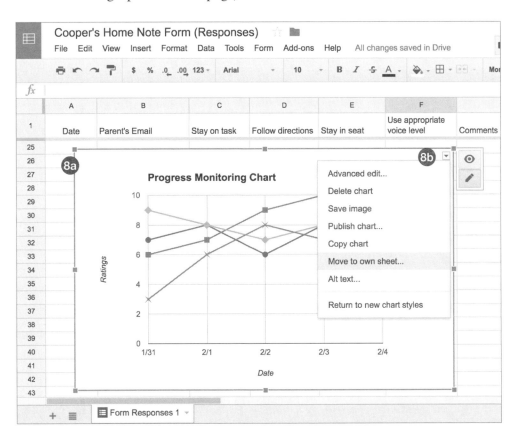

155

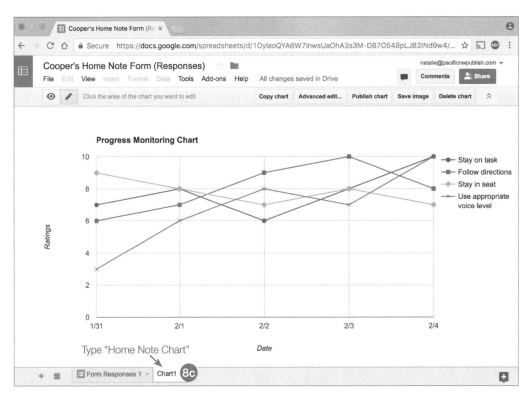

NOTE: You can move back and forth between the pages in the sheet by clicking on the tabs at the bottom of the sheet.

How to Share Data and Personalize the Electronic Home Note (OPTIONAL)

O nly the interventionist or teacher-interventionist has access to the complete history of behavior ratings data and comments in Google Sheets.

Share the Data

If you wish to share that information with the classroom teacher, follow the steps below—first ensuring that you follow all district requirements in regard to confidentiality. **NOTE:** The teacher will need a Google account to view the information.

_____ 1. Access your dedicated Electronic Home Notes Google Drive.

_____ 2. Double-click on the appropriate Google Sheet ( ) to open it (e.g., Cooper's Home Note Responses).

_____ 3. Click on the **Share** icon at top right. (A Share With Others box will pop up.)

_____ 4. Under **People**, enter the email addresses of everyone you want to share the document with.

_____ 5. **IMPORTANT:**
Select the
Pencil icon
from the
pull-down
list at right
and select
Can View.

_____ 6. Add a note.

_____ 7. Click on the blue **Send** button. (The recipient will receive an
email similar to the one shown in the bottom graphic).

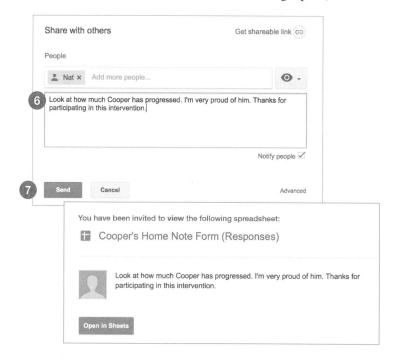

The recipient may get a You need permission popup box, in which case he
or she will need to click the **Request access** button and you will have to
grant permission.

Personalize the Electronic Home Note Form

During one of your meetings with the student, you may want to consider customizing the Electronic Home Note form to make it more personal and more motivating. You can add a picture, change the color theme, etc. The student can help design a custom border for the note. See the sample customized note shown in Figure 4.8a on the next page.

Follow the simple steps below or see Google Form instructions at http://support.google.com/docs/answer/2839737.

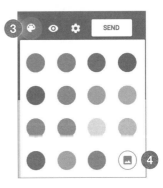

____ 1. Open the student's Form () from your Electronic Home Note Google Drive.

____ 2. Click on the **Color Palette** icon ( ) at top right. A box with several color selections will pop up.

____ 4. Choose from the range of colors or select the **More Themes** ( ) icon.

____ 5. If the student chose **More Themes** in Step 4, he or she can click on a theme from the list or click on **Upload photos** to select a personal photo.

____ 6. Click on the blue **Select** button once the student has selected a provided theme or uploaded a personal photo.

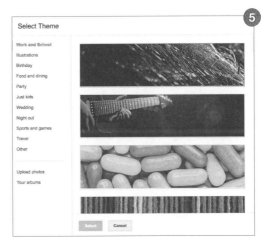

Figure 4.8a • Customized Home Note for Cooper

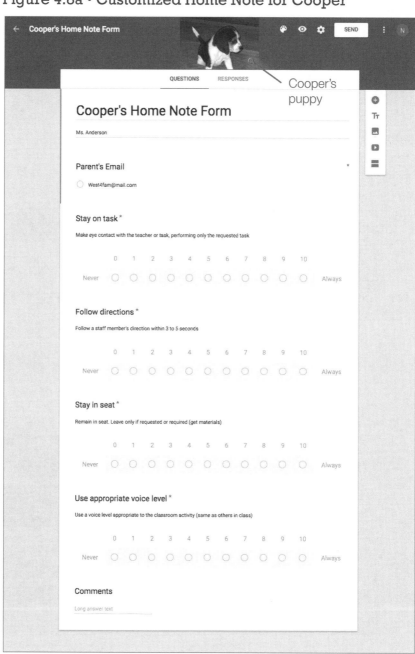

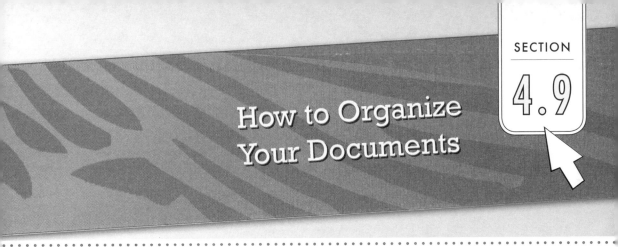

How to Organize Your Documents

I f you are an interventionist working with several students, once your program is up and running, it may be helpful to organize your files by classroom or teacher (e.g., M. Jones or Room 7). This section presents some ways to do that.

Create a Folder

_____ 1. Access your dedicated Electronic Home Notes Google Drive. (If a box with safe storage information appears, close it by clicking on the **x** in the upper right-hand corner.)

_____ 2. Click on **My Drive** to the right of the **New** button at the top and select **New folder**.

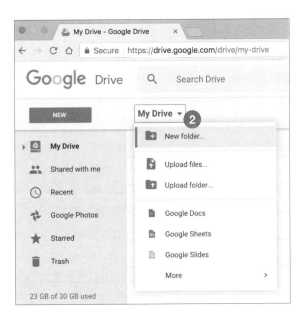

____ 3. In the New folder box, replace the highlighted text **Untitled folder** with a folder title (e.g.,"Room 5 Home Notes").

____ 4. Click the blue **Create** button.

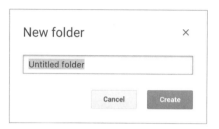

Move a File Into a Folder

____ 1. Highlight a file (e.g., a home note Form) by clicking on it.

____ 2. Select the **More actions** icon (⋮) in the menu bar at top right and select **Move to...**

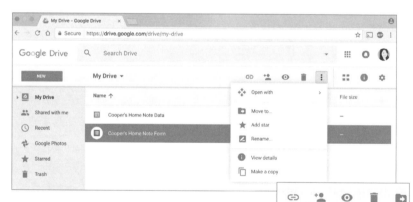

____ 3. To select the destination folder, do one of the following:

    a) Click on the arrow at the top to navigate up a folder.

    b) Double-click on an existing folder.

    c) Create a new folder by clicking on the folder icon at bottom right.

____ 4. Click on the blue **Move here** button.

SECTION 5

Connecting and Training

5.1 Networking: First Connections

- Preliminary Connections
- Complete Observations

5.2 Training: Final Setup and Teacher Consultation

- Teacher Training Meeting and Discussion of Final Setup Steps
- Cooper's Case Study, Teacher Consultation and Training Meeting

5.3 Training: Family Consultation

- Family Training Meeting
- Cooper's Case Study, Family Training Meeting

5.4   Training: Student Consultation

- Student Training Meeting
- Cooper's Case Study, Student Training Meeting

5.5   System Update: Follow-Up Observations

- Benefits of Follow-Up Observations
- How to Conduct Follow-Up Observations
- How to Use Follow-Up Observation Ratings
- Ready, Set, Go!

Networking

First Connections

Networking between the interventionist, teacher, and family is an important beginning to a successful Electronic Home Note program.

Objectives

- To obtain the teacher's permission for classroom observations

- To determine whether the teacher views Electronic Home Notes as a viable intervention option

- To obtain the family's permission for classroom observations

- To determine whether the family views Electronic Home Notes as a viable intervention option

Preliminary Connections

Meet Informally With the Referring Teacher (Interventionists)

The goal of this brief meeting is to gather preliminary information on the student's classroom behavior. Let the teacher know you look forward to working together. Explore the possibility of an Electronic Home Note intervention. If the teacher thinks a home note intervention might be helpful, move forward. If the teacher is not receptive to this intervention, look into other options. See Resources for other possibilities.

Teacher-Interventionist Chat Ask another staff member to conduct observations.

Set Up Classroom Observations

Set up two or three 15-minute classroom observations. Explain that you would like to collect on-task data on the student and peers for comparison. If possible, observe during times when behavior is most challenging.

Connect With the Family

Connect with the family to offer your support and request permission for observations. Let the family know you look forward to working together. Briefly explain Electronic Home Notes as a tool to create a positive and consistent feedback loop with the family. If the family is receptive, check to see whether the family has access to email via a computer, notebook computer, tablet, or smartphone. (If email isn't an option, explore the possibility of a paper home note. See Appendix B.) If the family does have email, you may wish to get the email address at this time. Be sure to double-check the email address so student information isn't mistakenly sent to the wrong address. Confidentiality is important!

■ Pop-Up Box

Next Steps

The remainder of Section 5 details the next steps—training the teacher and finalizing setup, training the family and training the student.

Complete Observations

Summarize information from completed observations on the Data Sharing form (Reproducible 5.1a). See Figure 5.1a on the next page.

See Section 3.1 for detailed information on classroom observations.

Figure 5.1a • Data Sharing Form

Electronic Home Notes

Data Sharing

Student __*Cooper West*__   Grade __*2*__

Classroom Teacher __*Mrs. Anderson*__

Observation Data Summary:

On-Task Data (referred student and same-sex peers)

Date *11/18* Activity *in-class math wksht*   Student % *50* / Peers % *80*

Date *11/19* Activity *in-class math wksht*   Student % *56* / Peers % *82*

Date *11/20* Activity *in-class math wksht*   Student % *48* / Peers % *79*

Averages: Student *51%* / Peers *80%*

29% Difference (Peers average minus student average)

Off-Task Behaviors Observed (referred student)

__*X*__ T = Talking out/Noise

__*X*__ O = Out of seat

_____ I = Inactive

__*X*__ N = Noncompliance

_____ P = Playing with an object

Notes:

Cooper is well-liked by his peers. He is distractible and distracting. Peer on-task behavior seems to be affected by Cooper's talking and out-of-seat behavior. May wish to enhance Cooper's on-task intervention by teaching planned ignoring of misbehavior by peers.

© 2017 William R. Jenson

REPRODUCIBLE 5.1a

Notes

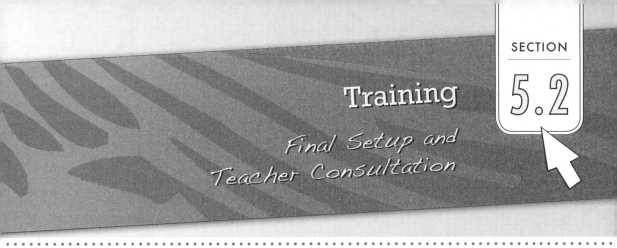

Training

Final Setup and Teacher Consultation

Buy-in from the adults who will be involved is necessary for a successful Electronic Home Note intervention. To begin the process of building an effective team, meet with the teacher again before meeting with the family and student.

Pop-Up Box

Team Building

Build a partnership with training and consultation as opposed to instruction and management.

Teacher-Interventionists

Now that your Electronic Home Note templates are set up, follow the steps on the Teacher Training and Setup Checklist (Reproducible 5.2a shown in Figure 5.2a on p. 172) to complete setup. No meeting is necessary because you are the teacher.

Interventionists

Once observations are complete, meet with the teacher using the Teacher Training and Setup Checklist (Reproducible 5.2a) as an agenda (see Figure 5.2a on page 172).

Objectives

Learn how to:

- Discuss (or review) student and peer data

- Discuss (or consider) academic skill deficits that may result in a "Can't Do" versus "Won't Do" problem

- Customize a practice Electronic Home Note, adding target behaviors, definitions, and goals

- Introduce (or review) the Electronic Home Note procedures

- Identify a schedule for rating behaviors

- Review (or plan for) Reward Days

- Practice with Electronic Home Notes

Materials Preparation

Program Materials

- Data Sharing form (Reproducible 5.1a) completed in advance
- Teacher Training and Setup Checklist (Reproducible 5.2a)
- Classroom Teacher's Checklist (Reproducible 5.2b)

Motivation System

Reproducibles selected from Section 3.4

Reproducible forms are available to download.

Electronic Forms and Equipment

- Set up Electronic Home Note

- Activate the Reward Day notification (all students on Electronic Home Notes will receive the Reward Day notification)

- Computer access (Step 5)

Teacher Training Meeting and Discussion of Final Setup Steps

Use the Teacher Training and Setup Checklist (Reproducible 5.2a) shown in Figure 5.2a on the next page as a guide for your meeting or next steps. A discussion of these steps follows.

1. **Welcome the teacher.**

2. **Discuss or review student data and the need for intervention.**

   Review the summarized data from observations and other information gathered to help identify target behaviors: Consider:

   - The percentage of time the student was on task versus peers during the same classroom activity

   - The types and frequency of behaviors observed when the student was off task (e.g. talking out, out of seat, etc.).

3. **Discuss or consider academic skills.**

   Discuss or consider whether academic skill deficits may indicate a "Can't do" instead of a "Won't do" problem. This framework will help you structure a successful intervention. Ask:

   - Is the student unable to carry out an assigned academic task due to a skill deficit that prompts off-task behavior? If yes, intervention should include academic supports.

   - Is the student able to carry out the assigned academic task but is unmotivated? If yes, this problem may be addressed via behavioral supports.

   - Is the student making a choice to engage in inappropriate behavior? If yes, this problem may be addressed via behavioral supports.

Figure 5.2a • Teacher Training and Setup Checklist

Electronic Home Notes

Teacher Training and Setup Checklist

☐ 1. Welcome the teacher.

☐ 2. Review and discuss student data and the need for intervention. (Use the Data Summary Form).

☐ 3. Discuss or consider academic skills.

☐ 4. (Optional) Briefly share the benefits of the Electronic Home Note program.

☐ 5. Identify and define target behaviors, and goals, and when the target behaviors will be rated.

Target Behavior 1 _____ Goal _____

Definition _____

When _____

Target Behavior 2 _____ Goal _____

Definition _____

When _____

Target Behavior 3 _____ Goal _____

Definition _____

When _____

Target Behavior 4 _____ Goal _____

Definition _____

When _____

Target Behavior 5 _____ Goal _____

Definition _____

When _____

☐ 6. Create and customize the student's Electronic Home Note by editing in and defining target behaviors. (Optional: Create an Electronic Home Note to practice with first.)

☐ 7. Review or explain the teacher's role in the classroom.
- Monitor the student.
- Rank the behaviors on the Electronic Home Note and send home.
- Provide the student with descriptive feedback.
- Send work samples with the student on Reward Days.

☐ 8. Review Reward Days and how they will be earned.

☐ 9. Develop comfort with the Electronic Home Note. (Practice.)

☐ 10. Identify a time to observe (or have another staff member observe) and rate the student on the priority goal. _____

© 2017 William R. Jenson

REPRODUCIBLE 5.2a

Figure 5.2b • Framework for Can't Do Versus Won't Do Problem

Can't Do Problem	Won't Do Problem
Academic Skill Deficit ⇩ Not completing work ⇩ Falling behind peers	**Lack of Motivation** ⇩ Not completing work ⇩ Falling behind peers

4. (Optional) **Briefly share the benefits of the Electronic Home Note program.** Suggested topics include:

   - School and home collaboration
   - Effectiveness research
   - Positive but consistent feedback loop with the family
   - Motivation to improve
   - Progress monitoring

5. **Identify and define target behaviors, goals, and when the target behaviors will be rated.**

   - Work with the teacher to select target behaviors and define what the behavior looks like during specific activities.

   - Explain that target behaviors will be rated on a scale of 0 to 10, with 0 representing *Never* (0%) and 10 representing *Always* (100%).

   - Set ambitious but achievable goals (see Sections 3.2 and 3.3).

■ **Pop-Up Box**

Goals

When a goal is met for 8 days out of 10, celebrate! A new goal can be set or the intervention faded. (See Section 7 for generalization and fading procedures.)

6. **Create and customize the student's Electronic Home Note.**

   (Optional for new users: Use practice documents as described in Item 9.) Use the information in Section 4.3 to customize the student's Electronic Home Note. (Do not link the Home Note to the spreadsheet until you've met with the family.) Review what the home note documents will look like and then:

- Edit in specific target behaviors based on observation data and the teacher's priorities.

- Edit in what the goal behavior should look like (e.g., On Task is described or defined as "Make eye contact with the teacher or task and perform the requested task").

- Identify a schedule for rating each behavior.

- Explain that rating the student at specific times leads to consistent, accurate, and reliable data. For example, a behavior might be rated all day, only in the morning or afternoon, or during specific times the student struggles with a behavior (e.g., during seatwork time, small group or whole class time, a specific subject, recess, or transitions.)

- Have the teacher save the Electronic Home Note to his or her desktop. Practice rating the student, but do not submit (send) the form.

7. Explain or review the teacher's responsibilities.

The teacher is responsible for rating the student's behaviors daily and sending the Electronic Home Note. Share the Classroom Teacher's Checklist (Reproducible 5.2b) shown in Figure 5.2b on the next page.

Each day the teacher will:

- Monitor the student during established times throughout the day.

- Complete and send the Electronic Home Note.

- Provide the student with positive descriptive feedback.

Figure 5.2b • Classroom Teacher's Checklist

Electronic Home Notes

Classroom Teacher's Checklist

Monday

☐ 1. Monitor the student during established times throughout the day.

☐ 2. Provide the student with positive descriptive feedback.

☐ 3. Complete the Electronic Home Note ratings.

☐ 4. Add comments to the home note and send.

Tuesday

☐ 1. Monitor the student during established times throughout the day.

☐ 2. Provide the student with positive descriptive feedback.

☐ 3. Complete the Electronic Home Note ratings.

☐ 4. Add comments to the home note and send.

Wednesday

☐ 1. Monitor the student during established times throughout the day.

☐ 2. Provide the student with positive descriptive feedback.

☐ 3. Complete the Electronic Home Note ratings.

☐ 4. Add comments to the home note and send.

Thursday

☐ 1. Monitor the student during established times throughout the day.

☐ 2. Provide the student with positive descriptive feedback.

☐ 3. Complete the Electronic Home Note ratings.

☐ 4. Add comments to the home note and send.

Friday

☐ 1. Monitor the student during established times throughout the day.

☐ 2. Provide the student with positive descriptive feedback.

☐ 3. Complete the Electronic Home Note ratings.

☐ 4. Add comments to the home note and send.

Reward Days

☐ Save academic work samples to review on Reward Days. (Send samples with the student to the interventionist.)

© 2017 William R. Jenson

REPRODUCIBLE 5.2b

- Add comments.

   Model how to provide "success" comments such as "Wow! Cooper met his on-task goal 2 days in a row." Or "Cooper got a 9 on his on-task goal. He exceeded his goal of 8. Thank you for your help."

   Model "try again" comments such as, "On-task was harder today, but I'm confident Cooper will be back on track tomorrow." Or "Cooper followed directions all morning. Tomorrow I'm confident he can work on following directions in the afternoon." The goal is to be honest but downplay unsuccessful days.

On Reward Days, the teacher will also:

Send (or review) academic work samples with the student so the interventionist can review the student's work, celebrate improvements, and problem-solve as needed.

8. Review Reward Days and how they will be earned.

Explain the motivation components of *The Tough Kid Electronic Home Notes* program that you've selected for the student. Select the target behavior and goal that will be tied to Reward Days.

9. Develop comfort with the Electronic Home Note (practice).

Invite questions. To ensure a successful intervention, interventionists and teachers should be comfortable with the steps for completing and sending the Electronic Home Note.

10. Identify a time to observe (or have another staff member observe) and rate the student on the behavioral goal.

Follow-up procedures include an observation during the first week of the intervention. During the observation, the student is rated independently by both the observer and teacher. This follow-up observation allows the teacher and interventionist (or another staff member) to compare ratings and troubleshoot as needed. (See Section 7.1 for additional information.)

Cooper's Case Study, Teacher Consultation and Training Meeting

Mr. James and Ms. Anderson meet and work through the Teacher Training Checklist. Ms. Anderson shares academic work samples with Mr. James. Cooper's math work shows that he is able to do his math problems correctly but fails to finish his work—a Won't Do problem.

After reviewing the suggested reward system, Ms. Anderson expresses optimism. Cooper enjoys games and has been motivated when rewards were available. (See Cooper's Case Study box on the next page.)

While working together with Ms. Anderson, Mr. James customizes Cooper's Practice Home Note following the steps in Section 4 and Appendix A (How to Practice).

- Mr. James and Ms. Anderson customize the Practice Home Note with Cooper's proposed behavior targets and descriptions. (For this practice session, they use Mr. James's nondedicated email address for the parent's email address.)

- Once the Practice Home Note and data collection spreadsheet have been linked, Mr. James sends the home note to Ms. Anderson.

- Ms. Anderson drags the Practice Home Note to her desktop, opens it, rates the student, and submits it.

- Mr. James opens his email, and Ms. Anderson views the note he received in his nondedicated email. Then, role-playing the parent, he sends a reply.

- Next, Mr. James shows Ms. Anderson the Reward Day notification that he receives in the role-play.

After practicing a couple of times, Ms. Anderson feels confident in the process and ready to meet with Cooper's parents.

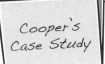

Rating Scale and Goals Review

Teacher Training Meeting: Ms. Anderson

Proposed Target Behaviors

1. On Task: Make eye contact with the teacher or task. Perform only the requested task.
   When: Math independent work   Goal: 7/10 (70%)

2. Follow Directions: Follow a staff member's directions in 3 to 5 seconds.
   When: Math independent work   Goal: 7/10 (70%)

3. Stay in Seat: Remain in seat. Leave only if requested or required (getting materials).
   When: Math independent work   Goal: 7/10 (70%)

4. Appropriate Voice Level: Use a voice level appropriate to the classroom activity (same as others in class).
   When: Math independent work   Goal: 7/10 (70%)

Reward Goal: On Task and Reviewing Home Note With Parent

Motivation System: Reward Days, Reward Menu with Chart Moves and spinner

Training

Family Consultation

A collaborative relationship between families and the school is crucial to fostering positive student behaviors. Increased school-home collaboration and communication allow greater access to resources and information for both the family and the school and help students generalize behaviors across settings. Once the Electronic Home Note has been customized, meet with adult family members (parents, caregivers, guardians).

Objectives

Goals for this meeting are to:

- Build a foundation for collaboration
- Review the target behaviors and goals identified by the teacher and interventionist
- Introduce Electronic Home Notes and procedures
- Explain Reward Days
- Review the family's role during the program
- Promote buy-in and enthusiasm

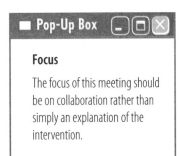

■ Pop-Up Box ☐☐☒

Focus

The focus of this meeting should be on collaboration rather than simply an explanation of the intervention.

Materials Preparation

Program Materials

- Data Sharing form (Reproducible 5.1a) completed in advance
- Family Training Checklist (Reproducible 5.3a)
- Family's Checklist (Reproducible 5.3b) with who, where, and when to meet for Reward Days filled in

Reproducible forms are available to download.

Electronic Forms and Equipment

- Computer access
- Setup of the Student's Electronic Home Note customized with the proposed target behaviors accessible for reviewing and editing
- Sample Reward Day notification

Family Training Meeting

Use the Family Training Checklist (Reproducible 5.3a) shown in Figure 5.3a on the next page as a guide for your meeting. A discussion of these steps follows.

1. **Welcome the family. Discuss strengths and needs.**

   Express your appreciation to the family for their willingness to meet and collaborate. Discuss the student's strengths as well as areas for development. Invite the family members' participation.

2. **Discuss proposed target behaviors and goals and modify as appropriate.**

   Briefly share the results of observations and the target behaviors, their definitions, and goals. Explain that these goals are obtainable for the student. Invite the family's participation and modification of target behaviors and goals.

Figure 5.3a • Family Training Checklist

Electronic Home Notes

Family Training Checklist

☐ 1. Welcome the family. Discuss student strengths and needs.

☐ 2. Discuss proposed target behaviors and goals, and modify as appropriate.

☐ 3. Introduce the Electronic Home Note program.

☐ 4. Demonstrate how the teacher will use the Electronic Home Note to rate the target behaviors. Show an example of the home note email.

☐ 5. Explain the Reward Day and Reward Day notifications.

☐ 6. Review the family's role, sharing the Family's Checklist.

☐ 7. Share the motivation system and discuss possible rewards.
Possible rewards:

_____   _____

_____   _____

_____   _____

_____   _____

☐ 8. Invite collaboration.

© 2017 William R. Jenson

REPRODUCIBLE 5.3a

IMPORTANT NOTE: If you add a behavior instead of editing one, create a new Electronic Home Note after the meeting. Behavior targets will appear in the data collection spreadsheet and email in the order they are created, regardless of how they appear on the screen.

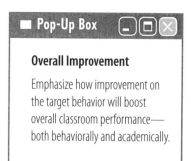

Pop-Up Box

Overall Improvement

Emphasize how improvement on the target behavior will boost overall classroom performance—both behaviorally and academically.

3. **Introduce the Electronic Home Note program and its procedures.**

   Show the Electronic Home Note to the family members. Discuss any edits that will be made based on the family's feedback. Make sure that you have the family's preferred email address.

4. **Demonstrate how the teacher will use the Electronic Home Note to rate the target behaviors.**

   Explain that target behaviors will be rated on a scale of 0 to 10, with 0 representing *Never* (0%) and 10 representing *Always* (100%).

   Create sample ratings and comments, but do not send (submit) the email.

   Review a sample Electronic Home Note with the family members. Point out the ratings and the Comments sections. (See Figure 5.3b on the next page.)

5. **Explain Reward Days and Reward Day notifications.**

   Explain that Reward Days will occur two to three times each week. Show the family a Reward Day notification and explain that a notification will be sent randomly to their email address after a family member has reviewed the note with the student and sent a reply to the interventionist. Make sure the family knows how to send a reply email, and review what the Reward Day notification looks like. (See Figure 5.3b on the next page.)

Figure 5.3b • Sample Electronic Home Note and Reward Day Notification

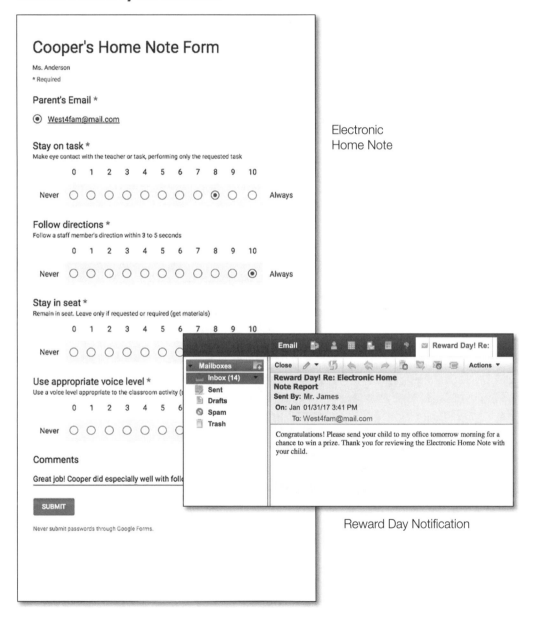

Electronic Home Note

Reward Day Notification

6. Review the family's role.

Explain family members' responsibilities using the Family's Checklist (Reproducible 5.3b shown in Figure 5.3c). Provide the family with a copy of the checklist.

The family's regular involvement and encouragement are major components in fostering the child's improved behavioral skills at school and in generalizing the skills to other settings. Emphasize the importance of reviewing the Electronic Home Note ratings with the child every day and providing positive descriptive feedback.

Coach the parent on how to provide positive and constructive feedback based on the ratings. Table 5.3a provides some sample language for at-home discussions.

Table 5.3a • Positive Parent Comments

Ratings	Example Comments
Good	• Great job today! All your ratings were amazing! • Your teacher thought you did very well today. I like all of these high ratings. • I'm very proud of you for all of your great ratings! • You must have worked hard to stay on task.
So-So	• Your ratings are OK, but tomorrow I know you can get higher ratings. • Your teacher and I know you can get higher ratings. • Remember when you got higher ratings? What was different about that day?
Inconsistent	• You did so well with completing your work. What can you do tomorrow to use an appropriate voice level? • I know tomorrow you will follow directions as well as you stayed on task today. • I'm proud that you kept your hands to yourself today. Tomorrow I would like you to work on being on task.
Poor	• Today wasn't as good as all your great days. How was today different from when you have good days? • Your teacher and I know you have a way of putting this day behind you and making tomorrow great!

Figure 5.3c • Family's Checklist

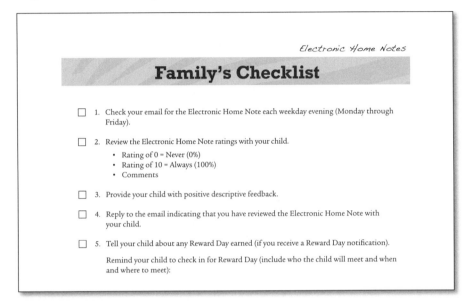

Electronic Home Notes

Family's Checklist

☐ 1. Check your email for the Electronic Home Note each weekday evening (Monday through Friday).

☐ 2. Review the Electronic Home Note ratings with your child.
- Rating of 0 = Never (0%)
- Rating of 10 = Always (100%)
- Comments

☐ 3. Provide your child with positive descriptive feedback.

☐ 4. Reply to the email indicating that you have reviewed the Electronic Home Note with your child.

☐ 5. Tell your child about any Reward Day earned (if you receive a Reward Day notification).

Remind your child to check in for Reward Day (include who the child will meet and when and where to meet):

Families are busy. Let them know that you understand. The Electronic Home Note can be reviewed with the child in 2 to 3 minutes. Assist families in scheduling time to review and discuss the home note.

Share ideas for when to review home notes:

- During snack time. Set the tone by letting the child choose a snack. Find a calm, quiet spot to enjoy the snack and review the Electronic Home Note.

- Before designated TV time, give your child the option of reviewing the note during the first or second commercial break. Mute the television or move to another room to review the note.

■ Pop-Up Box ⊟⊡⊠

Busy Families

Families are busy. Help with specific tips for reviewing the home note regularly.

7. **Share the motivation system and discuss possible rewards.**

Share the motivational strategies incorporated into the program. Show the family the Chart Moves Board, reward spinner, and Mystery Motivator.

Have family members suggest possible rewards that their child could earn. Explain that the rewards will be provided at school and ask the family to refrain from providing tangible rewards at home.

8. **Invite collaboration.**

Ask the family if they have any questions. Be sure to let them know that you are available to assist them at any time and make certain that they have your current contact information.

Cooper's Case Study, Family Training Meeting

Mr. James and Ms. Anderson meet with the family and work through the Family Training Checklist. Cooper's mother agrees that the target goals will be good for Cooper. On Task is selected as the reward or priority goal. The group also discusses homework, and Ms. Anderson agrees to add homework assignments to the Comments section of the Electronic Home Note.

Cooper's mom expresses appreciation when given coaching on how to respond to the home note ratings. She shares that her tendency is to focus on problems instead of successes.

See File 5.3a on the next page for details of the Family Consultation and Training Meeting.

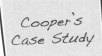

Family Consultation and Training Meeting

Meeting: Present—Mrs. West (Cooper's mom), Ms. Anderson (classroom teacher), Mr. James (interventionist)

Proposed Target Behaviors

1. On Task: Keep eye contact with the teacher or task. Perform only the requested task.
    When: Math independent work   Goal: 7/10 (70%)

2. Follow Directions: Follow a staff member's directions in 3 to 5 seconds.
    When: Math independent work   Goal: 7/10 (70%)

3. Stay in Seat: Remain in seat. Leave only when requested or required (getting materials, transitioning to and from small group).
    When: Math independent work   Goal: 7/10 (70%)

4. Appropriate Voice Level: Use a voice level appropriate to the classroom activity (same as others in class).
    When: Math independent work   Goal: 7/10 (70%)

Comment section: Ms. Anderson will list any homework for the evening and when it is due.

Motivation System: Reward Days, Chart Moves, spinner, Reward Menu, Mystery Motivator

Rewards Suggested: Magic tricks, time to play basketball, cookie snacks

Notes

Training

Student Consultation

Student training meetings are necessary for effective implementation of the Electronic Home Note program. Student motivation is paramount for behavioral change throughout the program and for generalization to other settings. This section covers how to conduct the initial student training and consultation meeting.

Objectives

The goals of the initial student meeting are to:

- Introduce the overall goals of the Electronic Home Note program

- Introduce and have the student practice target behaviors and how to be successful

- Introduce the Electronic Home Note and how the teacher will rate the student

- Introduce the Self-Plotting Graph and goal

- Explain Reward Days and the motivation system

- Reward the student for participation

- Build ownership of the program with student feedback

Materials Preparation

Program Materials

- Student Training Checklist (Reproducible 5.4a)
- Self-Plotting Graph (Reproducible 3.6a)
- Fun-O-Meter or Student Feedback Form (Reproducible 3.6b or 3.6c)
- Reward Menu (Reproducible 3.4b)
- Chart Moves Board (Reproducible 3.4d)
- Sample Reward Day notification

Reproducible forms are available to download.

Other Materials

- Invisible-ink pens
- Rewards
- Access to online spinner

Electronic Forms and Equipment

- Setup of the student's Electronic Home Note customized with the proposed target behaviors
- Computer access

Student Training Meeting

Use the Student Training Checklist (Reproducible 5.4a) shown in Figure 5.4a on the next page as a guide for this meeting.

1. **Welcome the student.**

   Welcome the student and explain that you are meeting to talk about a program that will assist him or her in increasing positive classroom behaviors. Explain that the program will allow the student to do better on schoolwork, enjoy class, and earn rewards while learning new skills.

Figure 5.4a • Student Training Checklist

Electronic Home Notes

Student Training Checklist

- ☐ 1. Welcome the student.
- ☐ 2. Introduce the Target Behaviors.
- ☐ 3. Introduce the Electronic Home Note.
- ☐ 4. Introduce the Self-Plotting Graph and Target Goal.
- ☐ 5. Explain Reward Days and the Motivation System.
- ☐ 6. Reward the student for participation.
- ☐ 7. Have the student fill out a feedback form.

2. Introduce the target behaviors.

Introduce the target behaviors that were developed by the interventionist, teacher, and adult family members. Explain that the teacher and family think these behaviors are important to help the student be successful.

- Have the student demonstrate the target behaviors.

- If the student does not or cannot appropriately demonstrate the behaviors, model what each behavior should look like. Then have the student try again.

- Continue role-playing as needed using examples and non-examples to define and operationalize behaviors for the student.

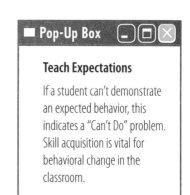

■ Pop-Up Box

Teach Expectations

If a student can't demonstrate an expected behavior, this indicates a "Can't Do" problem. Skill acquisition is vital for behavioral change in the classroom.

191

- Check for understanding by having the student role-play the appropriate target behavior without your assistance.

3. **Introduce the Electronic Home Note.**

Show the student the Electronic Home Note and explain how the teacher will rate the target behaviors.

- Rating of 0 = Never (0%)
- Rating of 10 = Always (100%)

Optional: Allow the student to suggest pictures for the Electronic Home Note (see Section 4.8).

Show the student an example of the behavioral ratings in a family email.

4. **Introduce the Self-Plotting Graph and target goal.**

Show the student a Self-Plotting Graph (Reproducible 3.6a). See Figure 5.4b on the next page. Write the goal for the target behavior on the graph. Help the student draw in a goal line. Explain that the student's family, teacher, and interventionist are confident that the student can achieve the goal and that you and the student will meet regularly so he or she can plot the progress.

NOTE: You will teach the student how to plot ratings on the first Reward Day.

5. **Explain Reward Days and the motivation system.**

Explain that Reward Days are the days when you will meet and review the student's progress and also reward the student for working on the goals. Discuss how Reward Days will occur randomly a few times each week. A chance to earn the Reward Day will occur when the student and family review the Electronic Home Note.

Figure 5.4b • Self-Plotting Graph

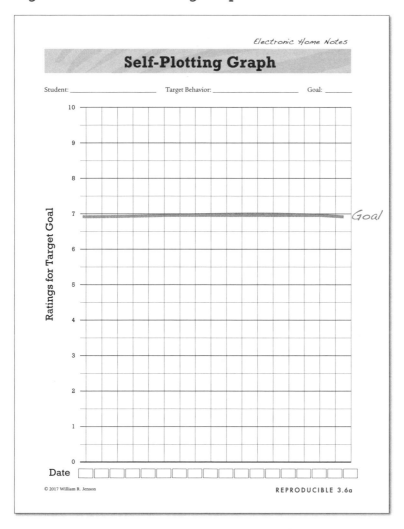

Show the student the reward spinner, Reward Menu, Mystery Motivators, Chart Moves Boards and other motivational components you've decided to use. Have the student help identify items to include on the Reward Menu.

Show the student a Reward Day notification. Explain when and where you will meet on Reward Days.

6. Reward the student for participation.

For immediate buy-in, reward the student for participating in the meeting by having the student use the motivational components you've selected. For example, have the student spin an electronic spinner or throw a die to earn a Mystery Motivator.

7. Have the student fill out a feedback form.

For younger students use the Fun-O-Meter and for older students the Student Feedback Form (Reproducibles 3.6b and 3.6c, respectively) to build ownership in the program.

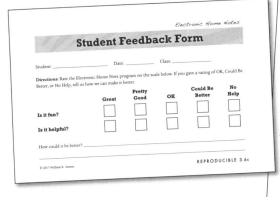

- Have the student fill out the appropriate form to rate his or her experience during this introductory meeting.

- Troubleshoot any concerns the student might have. (See Section 7.3 for additional information.)

Cooper's Case Study, Training Meeting

After meeting with Ms. Anderson and Mrs. West (Cooper's mother), Mr. James meets with Cooper to review and practice his target behaviors. Cooper is positive about Chart Moves, the online spinner, and the Mystery Motivator.

Cooper indicates he likes Snickers and Tootsie Rolls. Mr. James provides other suggestions and helps Cooper finalize his initial Reward Menu. Mr. James lets Cooper spin the online spinner as a reward for his cooperation. Cooper wins a Mystery Motivator and gets to select an inexpensive toy. Mr. James lets Cooper know the Mystery Motivator is a mystery so they will never know what's inside it until it is opened. Cooper fills out the Fun-O-Meter, indicating that he enjoyed his first session with Mr. James.

Electronic Home Notes

Reward Menu

1. Tootsie Roll
2. Snickers Bar
3. Pencil
4. Ball monitor for the day
5. New magic trick
6. Mystery Motivator

© 2017 William R. Jenson

REPRODUCIBLE 3.4b

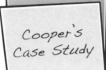

Cooper's Case Study

Student Consultation and Training Meeting

Cooper was introduced to his behavioral goals, the Chart Moves Board, and online spinner. Cooper practiced his target behaviors and was able to demonstrate the ability to do each. Appropriate voice level required modeling and practice.

Cooper reviewed the Electronic Home Note, the home note email, and the Self-Plotting Graph.

Motivation System: Chart Moves, use of online spinner, Mystery Motivator
Rewards Menu: 1) Snickers Bar, 2) Tootsie Roll, 3) 5 minutes with a friend, 4) 5 minutes of basketball, 5) Learn magic trick, 6) Mystery Motivator

Reward Days: Cooper will meet Mr. James in his office before school the day after a Reward Day notification is received.

Next Steps

Mr. James lets Ms. Anderson and Mrs. West know they are ready to begin. (Section 6 covers the steps for the first week of the Electronic Home Notes intervention.)

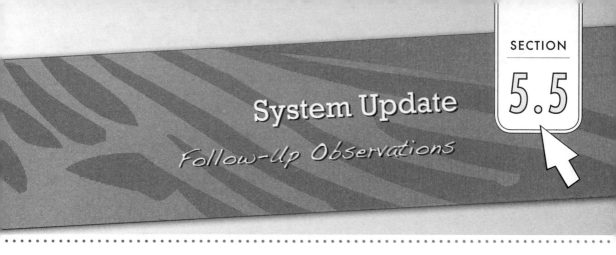

System Update

Follow-Up Observations

A follow-up classroom observation is recommended during the first week of implementation to ensure the intervention has a successful start. Best practice suggests scheduling observations once each week across the next several weeks.

Objectives

The goals of this section are to:

- Review the benefits of follow-up observations

- Learn how to use tools for follow-up observations

- Review how to use information from follow-up observations

Benefits of Follow-Up Observations

Follow-up observations allow you to validate whether the student is making progress toward goals as well as academic progress. These observations also provide an opportunity to monitor the similarity of an observer's ratings to the teacher's ratings and to check on program fidelity.

Challenging Students

Teacher-Interventionists: You may wish to invite another staff member to assist you with follow-up observations. Observations may help you rate with objectivity in the specified time period and assist you in motivating a challenging student to make improvements.

How to Conduct Follow-Up Observations

Monitor the student's target behavior with the Follow-Up Observation Form (Reproducible 5.5a) as follows.

1. **Select the target behavior or behaviors to be observed in the classroom.**

2. **Review the definition of the target behaviors to be observed in the classroom.** The observer needs to use the same definition as the teacher.

3. **Observe the student at the same time the teacher rates the student.** The observer should observe for at least 15 minutes.

4. **After the observation period, rate the student's target behaviors on a 0–10 scale.** Record ratings on the Follow-Up Observation Form. Have the teacher rate the student's target behavior on the Electronic Home Note. Record the teacher's score on the form for comparison.

5. **Compare and discuss the observer's ratings with the teacher's ratings of the student's target behaviors.** Discuss the inter-rater reliability with the teacher. See Figure 5.5a on the next page for a sample Follow-Up Observation Form.

Behavior Observation Form

Another option for follow-up observations is to use the Behavior Observation Form (Reproducible 3.1a discussed in Section 3.1). This form allows the observer to gather data on the student and peers for comparison.

Figure 5.5a • Follow-Up Observation Form

Electronic Home Notes

Follow-Up Observation Form

Name _____

Date	Time Period	Target Behavior	Observer Rating 0–10	Teacher Rating 0–10	Rating Difference	Next Steps
3/21	Math	On Task	8	5	3	Review behavior definitions
3/22	Math	On Task	7	6	1	None

Date	Time Period	Target Behavior	Observer Rating 0–10	Teacher Rating 0–10	Rating Difference	Next Steps
3/21	Math	On Task	8	7	1	None
3/21	Math	On Task	8	8	0	None

Review definitions of your target behavior and check program fidelity if follow-up observation ratings differ by more than 2 points.

© 2017 William R. Jenson

REPRODUCIBLE 5.5a

How to Use Follow-Up Observation Ratings

Follow-up in the classroom by an outside observer can yield important data and observations. For example:

- If ratings are similar (within one point), you may wish to schedule less frequent observations (e.g., every other week).

- If ratings are discrepant, the teacher can work to develop objective ratings of the student's behavior. Discuss the target behavior definitions and key things to look for.

- Follow-up observations in the classroom can also be used to help with troubleshooting if the student has a downward trend in the data or if progress is flat.

Ready, Set, Go!

You are ready to implement the first week of the program. Section 6 provides a guide for the first week of the Electronic Home Notes intervention. You will read more about Reward Days, Self-Plotting, and Student Work Samples.

Then dive in. You are ready to follow the first week's guide.

SECTION 6

Implementation

Leveling Up

How to Conduct Reward Days

Reward Days serve many functions in The Tough Kid Electronic Home Note program. The informal meetings provide the student with adult support, ongoing progress monitoring, and a fun motivation system. **NOTE:** There are other motivation systems that can work well with the program.

This section provides information on how to run an effective Reward Day meeting with one or more students

Objectives

You will learn how to:

- Set up a Reward Day schedule

- Conduct an effective Reward Day

- Teach the student how to self-monitor

- Discuss academic work samples

The sequence for implementing a Reward Day system follows the chart shown in Figure 6.1a on the next page.

Figure 6.1a • Reward Day Sequence Flowchart

```
                    ┌──────────────────────────────┐
                    │     Day Before Reward Day     │
                    └──────────────────────────────┘
                                  ↓
┌──────────────────────────────────────────────────────────────────┐
│ Interventionist or teacher-interventionist turns on Reward Day     │
│ notification.                                                      │
└──────────────────────────────────────────────────────────────────┘
                                  ↓
┌──────────────────────────────────────────────────────────────────┐
│              Teacher sends Electronic Home Note.                    │
└──────────────────────────────────────────────────────────────────┘
                                  ↓
┌──────────────────────────────────────────────────────────────────┐
│        Family reviews Electronic Home Note email with child.       │
└──────────────────────────────────────────────────────────────────┘
                                  ↓
┌──────────────────────────────────────────────────────────────────┐
│                   Family sends reply email.                         │
└──────────────────────────────────────────────────────────────────┘
                                  ↓
┌──────────────────────────────────────────────────────────────────┐
│        Family receives automatic Reward Day notification.          │
└──────────────────────────────────────────────────────────────────┘
                                  ↓
                    ┌──────────────────────────────┐
                    │          Reward Day           │
                    └──────────────────────────────┘
                                  ↓
┌──────────────────────────────────────────────────────────────────┐
│                Student reports for Reward Day.                      │
└──────────────────────────────────────────────────────────────────┘
```

How to Set Up an Unpredictable Reward Day Schedule

Reward Days should occur on unpredictable days two to three times each week. This variability helps students work consistently to meet their goals. If you have more than one student on Electronic Home Notes, Reward Days can develop into an informal support group as students give each other high-fives for winning rewards and making progress toward their goals.

■ Pop-Up Box

Scheduling Tip

When setting up the schedule, be cognizant of your own meeting schedule.

Try to set up regular times to meet (e.g., before school, during recess, before lunch, etc.)

Sample Text for a Reward Day Notification

Congratulations! Your child has earned a Reward Day. Please remind your child to come to join me tomorrow for a Reward Day!

- *Fourth through sixth grade: Before school*
- *First through third grade: Morning recess—check in with your teacher first*

Set up the unpredictable Reward Day schedule in advance (see sample schedule below).

REWARD DAY SCHEDULE

	Monday	Tuesday	Wednesday	Thursday	Friday
WEEK 1		★		★	★
WEEK 2		★	★	★	
WEEK 3	★		★		★
WEEK 4	★	★	★		
WEEK 5		★	★		★
WEEK 6	★	★		★	
WEEK 7	★		★		★
— For Facilitator's Eyes Only —					

How to Conduct a Reward Day

Reward Days are triggered by turning on the Reward Day notification in your dedicated Gmail account (see Section 4.6). The notice must be turned on no later than the end of the school day on the day before a Reward Day is scheduled. This ensures that the family will receive the Reward Day notification as soon as they send a reply to the Electronic Home Note email. The Reward Day routine includes the following steps.

1. **Congratulate the student.**

   As soon as the student reports in for a Reward Day, congratulate the student for reviewing the Home Note email with his or her family.

2. Review the student's progress on the target behaviors.

Review the progress the student has made on the target behaviors. The student's Electronic Home Note spreadsheet will include all teacher ratings and comments.

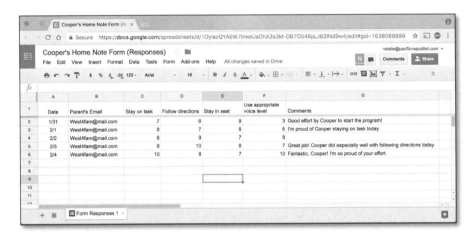

3. Review the student's academic work samples from the classroom.

Note successes. Help with difficulties and let the teacher know if the student is struggling with any required skills.

4. Have the student plot the Electronic Home Note ratings on a Self-Plotting Graph.

Have the student plot the Electronic Home Note ratings on a Self-Plotting Graph and compare his or her ratings with the goal line. See Section 6.2 for how to teach the student self-plotting.

5. **Complete steps in the student's motivation system. For example, have the student:**

- Color in half a box on a Chart Moves Board

- Spin a reward spinner for each dot uncovered on the Chart Moves Board

- Check the Reward Menu

- Collect the reward

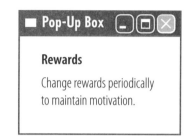

Rewards

Change rewards periodically to maintain motivation.

If the arrow lands on the spinner's Mystery Motivator wedge, hand the student the Mystery Motivator envelope and let the student tear it open.

6. **Remind the student to review the Electronic Home Note with his or her family every day.**

Let the student know tomorrow may be another Reward Day.

7. **Have the student mark the Fun-O-Meter (Reproducible 3.6b) or fill out the Student Feedback Form (Reproducible 3.6c).**

Use the student's feedback to discuss what was enjoyable and to problem-solve if needed.

Fading

Over time, you may want to reduce the frequency of the Reward Day from two or three times per week to only once per week. Fading is discussed in more detail in Section 7.5.

Mapping Progress
Self-Plotting

Self-plotting helps students take ownership of their progress. Students graph their Electronic Home Note ratings each Reward Day and look at how they compare with their goal.

Objectives

During the first week of implementation:

- To introduce self-plotting to the student
- To teach the student to self-plot and reflect on his or her data

How to Introduce Self-Plotting

Introduce the graph during the Student Training Meeting (see Section 5.4).

1. **Use the student's reward goal for self-plotting.**

2. **Show the graph to the student.** Say something like: *We're going to see how you can graph your progress so you know whether you are improving.*

3. **Have the student draw a goal line on the Self-Plotting graph.** Say something like: *Each Reward Day, you will graph your ratings. Your goal is a 7. Find the 7. Let's draw a line so you can see your goal.*

4. **Show the student three sample graphs that show flat data, data going down, and data going up.** Say something like:

   Look at these three graphs. This student scored a 4, 4, 4, 4, 4, and a 4. How did this student score? (8, 5, 4, 3, 2, 1)
   How did this student score? (5, 7, 8, 9, 9, 10)

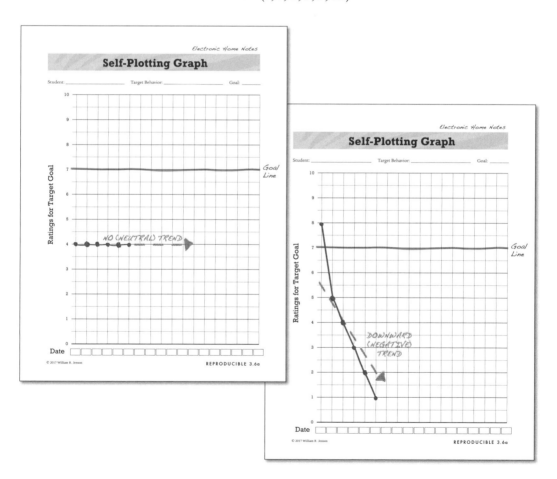

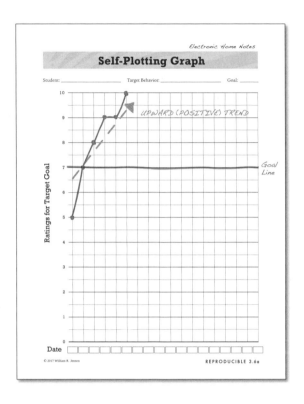

5. **Check for understanding.** Say something like:

If the line is going up, you are doing better! If the line is flat, you are staying the same. Which graph shows a student staying the same?

If the line is going down—uh, oh—you're having a hard time meeting your goal. Which graph shows a student who is having a hard time?

6. **Tell the student he or she will graph ratings each Reward Day and earn rewards for meeting or exceeding the goal.**

How to Graph Ratings and Discuss Goals

During subsequent Reward Day meetings, use self-plotting as a procedure to help the student focus on his or her progress.

1. **Have the student plot the first rating.** If the student met or exceeded the goal, congratulate the student. Discuss and practice how to improve.

2. **Check for understanding.** Say something like:

   If your line is flat, what does that mean? (I'm staying the same.)
   If your line is going down, what does that mean? (I'm having a hard time.)
   If your line is going up, what does that mean? (I'm doing better in class.)

Once older students are adept at graphing their priority or goal behavior, you may wish to teach them how to graph multiple target behaviors.

NOTE: More than one goal can be graphed on one chart if they all share the same goal line.

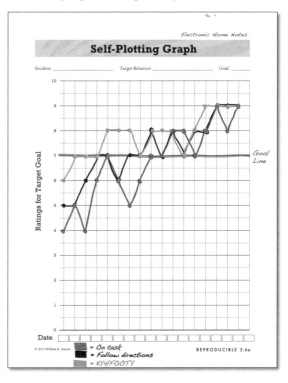

Classroom work samples allow you to highlight academic successes and diagnose academic difficulties. Each Reward Day, students need to bring work samples supplied by the teacher. Ask teachers to provide positive examples of work.

Objectives

This section provides procedures designed to:

- Focus on improvements in academic success

- Link behavioral success with academic success

- Troubleshoot academic problems

- Monitor progress

How to Use Classroom Work Samples

1. **Each Reward Day, ask the teacher to provide a positive (desired) example of work.**

   Monitor work from a specific subject area or instructional period. (If the teacher is rating during a specific subject or period, monitor work samples from that subject.)

2. **Praise the student for bringing a sample and provide positive descriptive feedback.**

   Descriptive feedback can help the student link his or her behavior with academic success. Say something like: *You did an excellent job answering every question! By staying on task, you are getting high marks in math.*

3. **Make notes on the quality of work.**

   If there is an academic problem, make a note to discuss instructional needs with the teacher as soon as possible or at your next scheduled meeting.

4. **Provide intermittent rewards for bringing the work sample.**

   Provide the student with social reinforcement for remembering to bring a work sample. For example, say something like: *Great job remembering your work! You make this so much easier for me. Thank you.* If the student forgets to bring a work sample, make a note to problem-solve with the teacher as soon as possible or at the next meeting.

5. **Make copies of the classroom work samples to document progress.**

   Make copies of work samples and keep them in the student's work file to document progress when you meet with the teacher or family.

Ready to Launch

Implementation Week 1

T he first week of implementation is the most important week of the
intervention. This section provides a step-by-step guide that will
help you work collaboratively with the teacher, parent, and student.
If you are a teacher-interventionist, this section will help ensure success
from the very beginning of your Electronic Home Note implementation.

With the teacher, family, and student, select a date to begin using the
Electronic Home Note program. Mondays are usually the best day for a
fresh start and to ensure a full 5 days before a weekend break.

Objectives

This guide to the first week will
help you to:

- Set up an unpredictable
  Reward Day schedule

- Establish effective routines

Materials Preparation

Schedule

- Set a date to begin using Electronic Home Notes.
- Set up an unpredictable Reward Day schedule.

Program Materials

- Electronic Home Note, Reward Day notifications, spreadsheet set up
- Self-Plotting Graph (Reproducible 3.6a)
   1 copy for the student
   3 copies with samples of flat, upward, and downward trend data
- Chart Moves Board (Reproducible 3.4d)

> **Reproducible forms** are available to download.

School Materials

- Envelope: add question mark to make a Mystery Motivator envelope
- Rewards on Reward Menu and Mystery Motivators
- Spinner (online or created from Reproducible 3.4c)
- Fun-O-Meter or Student Feedback Form (Reproducible 3.6b or 3.6c)
- Invisible-ink markers

Optional

- Program Materials: Behavior Observation Form (Reproducible 3.1a)
- School Materials: Timing device

First Day • Monday

1. Check in with the teacher and student.

Do a brief check-in to remind the teacher that it's the first day of the Electronic Home Note program.

- Refer to the Classroom Teacher Checklist to see if the teacher has any questions. Take this opportunity to remind the teacher to rate the target behaviors during the specified time period.

- Do a quick check to make sure the teacher still has easy access to the student's Electronic Home Note.

- Troubleshoot any new potential barriers and thank the teacher for participating in the program.

- Optional: Schedule a Follow-Up Observation for the middle of the week and a Follow-Up Meeting with the teacher for the end of the week (see Section 5.5).

Check in with the student for a quick pep talk. Remind the student that the teacher will send the first Electronic Home Note today. Review the student's reward system and responsibilities. Troubleshoot any potential barriers. Express confidence in the student's ability to meet the goals.

2. **Check in with the family.**

If possible, check in with the family before the end of the day. Let them know that this is the first day they will receive an Electronic Home Note email. Encourage them to review the ratings with the student and ask if they have any questions.

3. **Turn on the Reward Day notification.**

NOTE: A Reward Day notification will be sent only if the family emails to confirm their review of the Electronic Home Note.

4. **Check to see that teacher has completed and sent the Electronic Home Note.**

When the teacher sends the Electronic Home Note, you (the interventionist) will receive an email indicating the Electronic Home Note was sent (see Section 4.5b). Send a quick thank-you to the teacher.

5. **Watch for the family reply email.**

   If you do not receive a reply, check in by phone to make sure the Electronic Home Note email was received. (Remember that the reply email will go to the Gmail address associated with your dedicated Electronic Home Notes Google account.) The call can also serve as a prompt for a successful family review of the home note.

Second Day • Tuesday

1. **Turn off the Reward Day notification.**

   Turn off the Reward Day notification (vacation responder). If you leave it on, the next day will be a Reward Day.

2. **Record replies.**

   Keep a record of whether you received a reply email from the family.

3. **Meet with the student for the first Reward Day**. (Reward Day components should be ready to use before the meeting. See Section 6.1 for more information on Reward Days.)

   - Teach the student to self-plot the first rating. Access the student's spreadsheet to retrieve the ratings. Have the student draw the goal line (or review the goal line). Then have the student plot the first rating on the graph. Celebrate and discuss what the student did to achieve the goal, or discuss what the student can do in the future to reach it.

   - Implement the motivation system. For example, have the student color in spaces on the Chart Moves Board and spin the spinner if a dot is revealed. Provide the student with the associated reward.

   - Review the student's academic work.

- Congratulate the student for successes. Troubleshoot as needed.

- Ask the student to complete the Fun-O-Meter or Student Feedback Form. Review the student's feedback and problem-solve, if needed.

NOTE: If the family did not send an email reply to the Electronic Home Note, problem-solve with the student and family.

4. **At the end of the day, check in with the teacher.**

   If possible, check in to see if the teacher has any questions and make sure the Electronic Home Note has been sent. Optional: Remind the teacher that you will be conducting a Follow-Up Observation the next day (see Section 5.5).

5. **Watch for the family reply email and connect with the family.**

   When you receive the reply email, send a separate thank-you email letting the family know their participation is appreciated.

Third Day • Wednesday

1. **Turn on the Reward Day notification.**

2. **Optional: Conduct a Follow-Up Observation.**

   Conduct a Follow-Up Observation to assess the consistency of observer and teacher ratings. (See Section 7.1. You may also use the Classroom Teacher's Checklist to check fidelity [Section 5.2].)

3. **Check in with the family, teacher, and student.**

   Quick check-ins this first week will allow you to quickly troubleshoot, make adjustments, and promote success.

4. **Watch for the family reply email.**

Fourth Day • Thursday

At this point, things should be running smoothly based on feedback and your appropriate modifications. Check in with the family and teacher as needed.

1. **Leave the Reward Day Notification on.**

2. **Meet with the student for the second Reward Day.**

    - Have the student plot the first goal rating. Celebrate any improvements and discuss what the student did to meet the goal or improve, or discuss what the student can do to improve the rating. Practice any difficult behaviors or skills.

    - Implement the motivation system (e.g., Chart Moves Board, spin if a dot is uncovered, provide any reward earned).

    - Review the student's academic work.

    - Have the student fill out the Fun-O-Meter or Student Feedback Form.

    - Congratulate the student for successes. Troubleshoot as needed.

    NOTE: If the family did not send a response email, problem-solve with the student and family to help the student be successful next time (e.g., text reminders, adjust the rewards, etc.).

3. **Check that the teacher has completed and sent the Home Note.**

4. **Watch for the family reply email.**

Fifth Day • Friday

1. **Leave the Reward Day notification on.**

2. **Meet with student for the third Reward Day.**

   Continue bulleted activities from the fourth day, Thursday.

3. **Check that the teacher has completed and sent the Home Note.**

4. **Watch for the family reply email.**

5. **Congratulate all parties.**

   Send a quick email to all parties congratulating them for their joint efforts, and provide positive descriptive feedback.

Sample email note from an interventionist:

Dear [student name], [family member names], and [teacher],

It's been a great week! [Student name] had three fun Reward Days. [He/She] has already improved [his/her] on-task rating from a 5 to a 7.

Thank you, everyone!
[Interventionist]

Sample email note or comment from a teacher-interventionist:

Dear [student name] and [family member names]:

It's been a great week! [Student name] had three fun Reward Days. [He/she] has already improved [his/her] on-task rating from a 5 to a 7. I'm very proud of [student name].

Thank you all.
[Teacher]

Cooper's Case Study, The First Week

Cooper's first week on an Electronic Home Note is a success. By following the recommended procedures, Mr. James front-loads support, knowing that success is likely to breed success.

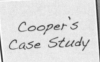

Cooper's Home Note Intervention Week 1

Monday · Day 1 (Reward Day notification on for Tuesday Reward Day)

Check-In: Ms. Anderson was ready to implement the Electronic Home Note. Cooper seemed positive and responded well to my check-in. Left a message on Mrs. West's cell phone reminding her that the Electronic Home Note would be in her email today.

Rating: Cooper's behavior in math showed a marked improvement.
Teacher Rating for On Task = 7 (70%)

Reply email received; Electronic Home Note reviewed with mom

Tuesday · Day 2
Reward Day (Reward Day notification off, no Reward Day on Wednesday)

Cooper was standing at our office eager for his Reward Day. I congratulated him for meeting his goal and got him started on his Self-Plotting Graph.

Cooper's Home Note Intervention, Week 1 (cont.)

Cooper colored in two triangles on his Chart Moves Board

- One for meeting his goal for On-Task behavior on Monday
- One for reviewing his Electronic Home Note with his mom

Rating: Cooper's on-task behavior in math was excellent.
Teacher Rating for On Task = 9 (90%)

Reply email received; Electronic Home Note reviewed with mom
Mom's comment: *Cooper is very excited about meeting his goal and so are we!*

Wednesday · Day 3
Not a scheduled Reward Day (Reward Day notification on for Thursday Reward Day)

Cooper stopped by my office even though it wasn't a Reward Day to let me know he got a 9 on his on-task goal. I congratulated him for his extraordinary efforts.

Classroom Observation: Ratings similar to Ms. Anderson
Rating: Cooper's on-task behavior in math was great.
Teacher Rating for On Task = 8 (80%)

Reply email received; Electronic Home Note reviewed with mom

(cont.)

Cooper's Home Note Intervention, Week 1 (cont.)

Thursday · Day 4
Reward Day (Reward Day notification on for Friday Reward Day)

Cooper was waiting at my door again. He completed his Self-Plotting Graph for Tuesday and Wednesday. He was enthusiastic when drawing a line from 7 to 9.

Cooper colored in two triangles on his Chart Moves Board

- One for meeting his goal for On-Task behavior on Wednesday
- One for reviewing his Electronic Home Note with his mom

Two dots were revealed on the Chart Moves Board.

Cooper spun the online spinner two times—earning either a Tootsie Roll or a magic trick. He chose the magic trick.

His Fun-O-Meter rating was again high.

Rating: Cooper's on-task behavior in math
Teacher Rating for On Task = 10 (100%)

Teacher's comment: *Wow! Cooper is really working hard! He finished his math in no time at all.*

Reply email received; Electronic Home Note reviewed with mom
Comment: *Cooper is so proud of himself.*

Cooper's Home Note Intervention, Week 1 (cont.)

Friday · Day 5
Reward Day (Reward Day notification off, no Reward Day on Monday)

Cooper plotted his Thursday score with ease on the Self-Plotting Graph (see Figure 6.4a). He was excited to plot his rating of 10. (I let him know that a 9 or 10 was exceptional and better than most kids.)

Cooper colored in two triangles on his Chart Moves Board

- One for meeting his goal for On-Task behavior on Wednesday
- One for reviewing his Home Note with his mom

One dot was revealed on the Chart Moves Board.

Cooper spun the online spinner and landed on the space for the Mystery Motivator. His prize was a LEGO figure. He was very excited and gave high marks on the Fun-O-Meter.

Rating: Cooper's on-task behavior in math
Teacher Rating for On Task = 9 (90%)

Email sent to Ms. Anderson, Mrs. West, and Cooper thanking them for their participation and congratulating Cooper on his great week.

Cooper's first week was exceptional. Mr. James and Ms. Anderson will stay in touch with Cooper's family, monitor progress, and adjust the system periodically to prevent lack of interest from developing.

Figure 6.4a • Sample Self-Plotting Graph

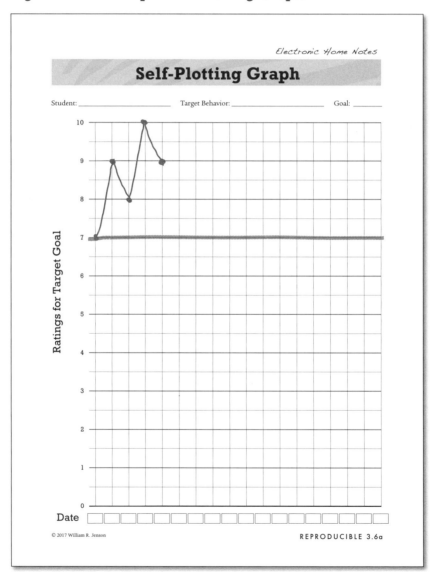

SECTION 7

Progress Monitoring and Follow-Up

7.3 Debugging the Program: Troubleshooting

- Resolving Student Behavioral Issues
- Resolving Issues With Family Follow-Through and Support
- Resolving Issues With a Teacher's Follow-Through and Support

7.4 Going Viral: Generalization

- Procedures for Generalizing Skills
- Next Step · Self-Monitoring
- Cooper's Case Study, Self-Monitoring

7.5 Going Offline: Fade the Program

- Options for Fading
- Cooper's Case Study, New Semester
- Cooper's Case Study, End-of-Year Recommendations

Analytics

Monitoring Data

An important component of an Electronic Home Note program is monitoring student progress so that decision making can be based on data.

Objectives

- To evaluate the student's responsiveness to the intervention

- To identify other factors potentially affecting the student's performance

- To make data-based decisions and modifications to the program

Teacher Ratings

The student's spreadsheet (Google Sheet) provides a quick view of the teacher's ratings for each target behavior. Data are presented by date and include ratings for each target behavior and the teacher's comments. See Figure 7.1a on the next page for a sample Electronic Home Notes spreadsheet.

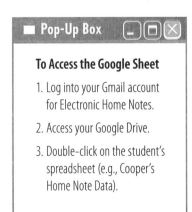

■ Pop-Up Box

To Access the Google Sheet

1. Log into your Gmail account for Electronic Home Notes.

2. Access your Google Drive.

3. Double-click on the student's spreadsheet (e.g., Cooper's Home Note Data).

Figure 7.1a • Home Note Data Spreadsheet

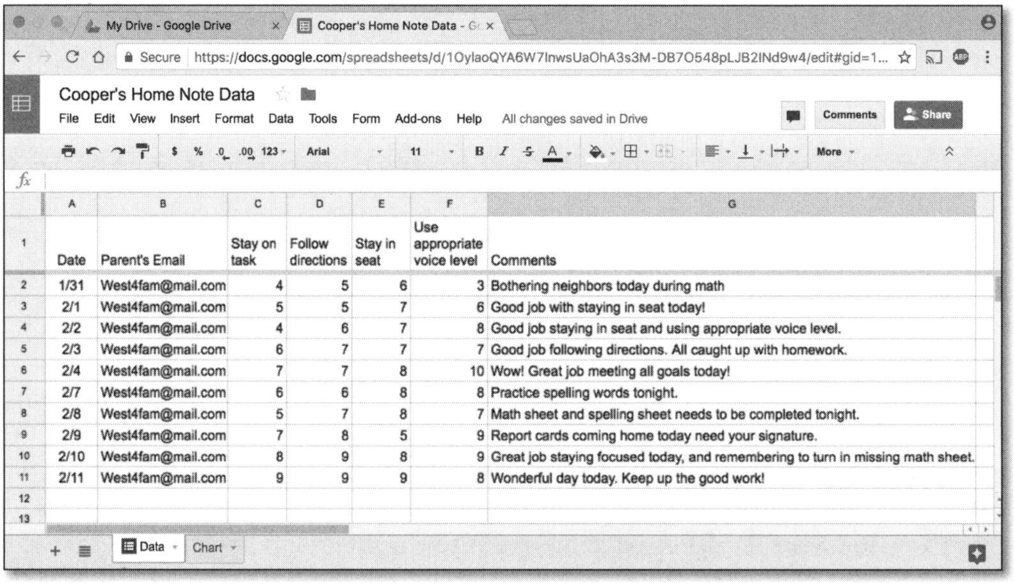

Cooper's Home Note Data

Date	Parent's Email	Stay on task	Follow directions	Stay in seat	Use appropriate voice level	Comments
1/31	West4fam@mail.com	4	5	6	3	Bothering neighbors today during math
2/1	West4fam@mail.com	5	5	7	6	Good job with staying in seat today!
2/2	West4fam@mail.com	4	6	7	8	Good job staying in seat and using appropriate voice level.
2/3	West4fam@mail.com	6	7	7	7	Good job following directions. All caught up with homework.
2/4	West4fam@mail.com	7	7	8	10	Wow! Great job meeting all goals today!
2/7	West4fam@mail.com	6	6	8	8	Practice spelling words tonight.
2/8	West4fam@mail.com	5	7	8	7	Math sheet and spelling sheet needs to be completed tonight.
2/9	West4fam@mail.com	7	8	5	9	Report cards coming home today need your signature.
2/10	West4fam@mail.com	8	9	8	9	Great job staying focused today, and remembering to turn in missing math sheet.
2/11	West4fam@mail.com	9	9	9	8	Wonderful day today. Keep up the good work!

Data Analysis

Analysis of the data will allow you to answer the following types of questions:

- How soon after implementing the Electronic Home Note program did changes in behavior occur?
- Is the student making adequate progress, even if the student has not consistently met the goals?
- Is the rate of progress acceptable?
- Should the student's goal be altered to reflect the student's current level of performance?
- Is it appropriate to begin fading the intervention?

Analyzing Graphs

A graph of student data provides a visual representation of the student's progress. A graph highlights changes or patterns in the data. Subtle changes in the data are difficult to detect in a spreadsheet.

Visual analysis of data includes looking for changes in trend, variability, and level.

 *Definitions*

lev·el

Relative amount of frequency of the target behavior (low, moderate, high)

trend

Direction of data over time (upward, downward, flat)

var·i·a·bil·i·ty

Amount of bounce in the data

With the Electronic Home Note program, you can use both the chart (see Figure 7.1b on the next page) generated by the spreadsheet (Google Sheet) and the student's Self-Plotting Graph.

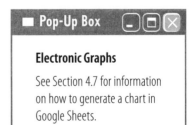

■ **Pop-Up Box**

Electronic Graphs

See Section 4.7 for information on how to generate a chart in Google Sheets.

Figure 7.1b • Home Note Data Chart

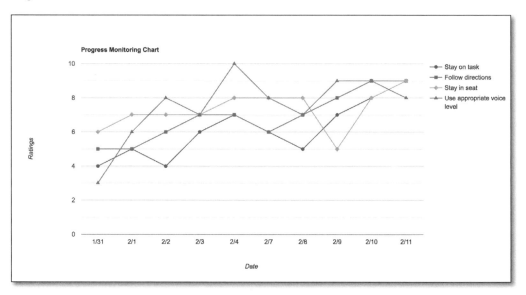

Trend

Use the student's Self-Plotting Graph or Electronic Home Notes chart to look for changes in the frequency of the target behavior over time. For example, a target behavior may gradually increase (upward trend), remain relatively unchanged (no trend), or gradually decrease (downward trend). These changes may not be noticeable on a day-to-day basis but apparent across time.

Trend lines drawn a on graph allow you to easily see the direction of the target data (see "How to Create a Trend Line" on the next page).

- **Upward (Positive) Trend.** An upward trend indicates an increase in the frequency of a behavior over time. An upward trend is desirable if the goal is stated positively (e.g., stay on task, follow directions, etc.). An upward trend indicates that the student is responding to the

How to . . .

CREATE A TREND LINE

1. Determine the mean (average) of the first three data points and graph that point.

$$8 + 6 + 5 = 19 \rightarrow 19 \div 3 = 6.3$$

2. Determine the mean of the last three data points and graph that point.

$$9 + 8 + 7 = 24 \rightarrow 24 \div 3 = 8$$

3. Draw a line connecting the two mean scores (the two points you just created) on the student's graph.

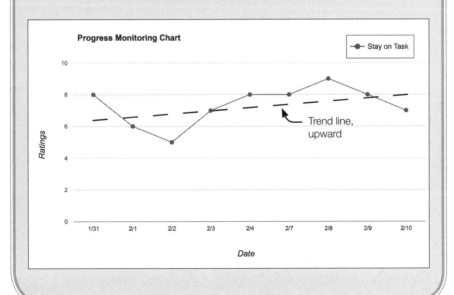

233

intervention and making progress. (See Section 3.2 for how to state a target behavior positively.)

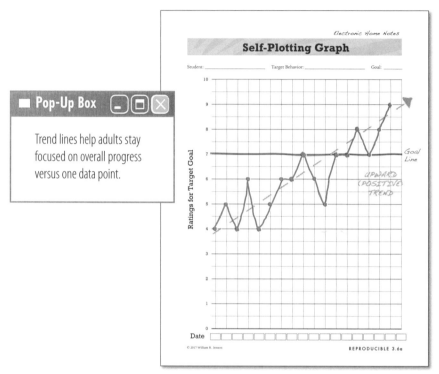

Pop-Up Box

Trend lines help adults stay focused on overall progress versus one data point.

Upward Trend

NOTE: A steep positive trend indicates that the student is quickly making progress whereas a more gradual trend means a slower rate of improvement.

- **No (Neutral) Trend.** Little to no change in the frequency of the target behaviors over time suggests

Pop-Up Box

Positively Defined Target Behaviors

Use positively defined target behaviors to promote positive behaviors. If you've inadvertently defined a negative target behavior (e.g., reduce shout-outs, don't disrupt others, etc.), an upward trend line is not desirable.

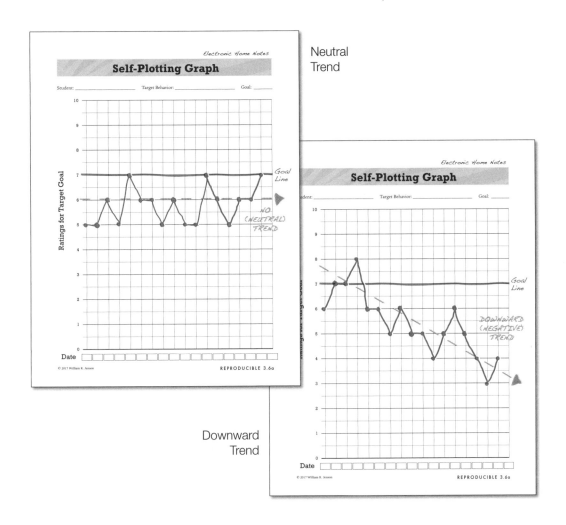

Neutral Trend

Downward Trend

a general lack of response or an inconsistent response to the Electronic Home Notes intervention. For neutral trends, assess program fidelity and elicit parent, teacher, and student feedback.

- **Downward (Negative) Trend.** A downward trend indicates a decrease in target behaviors over time. This pattern demonstrates that the frequency of a student's target behavior is declining and that something is impeding the student's success. For negative trends, assess program fidelity and elicit parent, teacher, and student feedback.

235

Variability (Bounce in the Data)

Look at the data for fluctuation or bounce. The consistency or inconsistency of ratings can signal how potent the Electronic Home Notes intervention is in changing the student's behaviors. Bounce in the data may indicate the presence of competing factors that influence the student's ability to change his or her behavior. For example, if Monday data are always low compared with other days, something that disrupts the student's progress may be occurring on weekends.

- **Low Data Bounce.** Low-bounce data are relatively consistent (i.e., data is usually within 1–2 points on the graph). Low-bounce data suggest that the intervention is effective and shows strong trends either upward or downward.

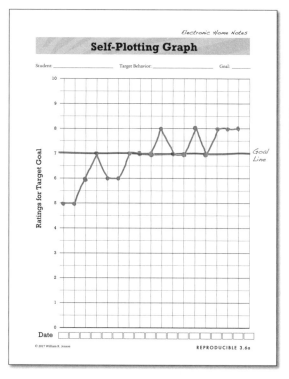

Low Data
Bounce
(Variability)

- **High Data Bounce.** High-bounce data regularly jump three or more points on the graph. High-bounce data suggest that unaccounted factors may be influencing the student's behavior and ability to make progress toward the goal. Use the data to determine possible factors for problem-solving.

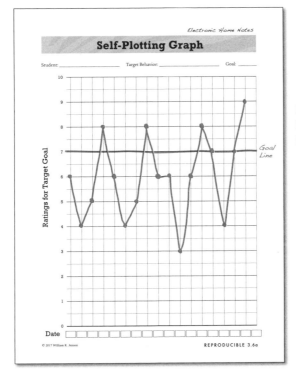

High Data
Bounce
(Variability)

Level

A review of the level provides a general analysis of the relative frequency of the student's target behavior. A rating from 0–4 might be considered very low to low frequency of the target behavior, while ratings from 6–10 might be considered high to very high frequency of the target behavior. Level provides general descriptors of behavioral change. For example: *In the first week of the Electronic Home Notes intervention, Jessica has gone from low rates of on-task behavior to high rates of on-task behavior.*

Example Data Level Classifications

Electronic Home Note Rating	Amount of Target Behavior
0–2	Very Low
2–4	Low
4–6	Moderate
6–8	High
8–10	Very High

Factors to Consider

Factors that may contribute to a neutral or downward trend in the student's progress include:

- Academic skill deficits (a Can't Do, not a Won't Do problem)
- External considerations, such as student's seat location in the classroom (distractions, too far away from the teacher, etc.)
- Problems with fidelity to the Electronic Home Note program
- Rewards: not sufficiently motivating, not given frequently enough
- Difficulties with peer interactions (e.g., bullying)
- Emotional or mental health concerns
- Factors in the home that contribute to difficulties at school

General Guidelines

After you summarize the student's data and review feedback with stakeholders (Section 7.2), determine whether to adjust the program.

As students demonstrate improved behavior and consistently meet their goals, revise expectations to reflect an increased performance standard. Guidelines include:

Adjust the program (troubleshoot and collaborate) when the trend in data is downward or neutral, a pattern of high bounce occurs in the data, and in general the data do not move toward high or very high ratings.

1. Increase goals only when the student is successful at least 8 out of 10 days.

2. Increase goals in 10% to 20% increments.

3. A maximum goal of 90% is appropriate for most behaviors.

4. Once the student has consistently met a goal of 90% in a variety of settings, consider beginning to fade the intervention (see Section 7.5).

Notes

Backing Up Your System

Follow-Up

Family members, teachers, and students should be asked to provide feedback to help improve the effectiveness and sustainability of the Electronic Home Note program. Ongoing consultation with stakeholders will benefit the current student as well as students with whom the program is used in the future. The greater the investment and involvement of stakeholders, the greater the buy-in and success of the intervention.

Objectives

- To gather feedback from the student, teacher, and family
- To review progress with the student, teacher, and family
- To make data-based decisions for next steps

Feedback From Participants

Student Feedback and Consultation

Student feedback is invited on a regular basis. During each Reward Day, students complete a feedback form. If a student marks *Could Be Better* or *No Help*, the student and interventionist discuss ways to improve the program. See Figure 7.2a on the next page.

Figure 7.2a • Feedback Forms

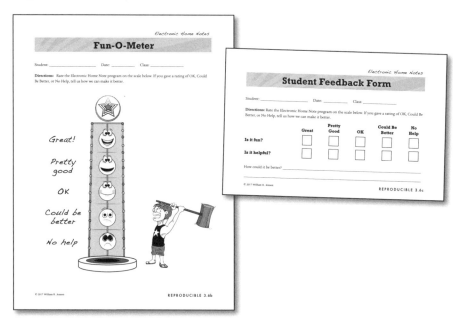

Teacher Feedback and Consultation

There are several options for connecting with teachers to solicit feedback, prevent problems from occurring, problem-solve, and acknowledge accomplishments.

- Informal check-ins each day throughout Week 1 (Section 6.4)

- Follow-up observations during Week 1 and once a week thereafter (Section 5.5)

- Short, informal meetings approximately once each week

- Family/Teacher Feedback Form (Reproducible 3.6d shown in Figure 7.2b)

- Meeting with the interventionist and family once every 3 to 4 weeks

Family Feedback and Consultation

There are several options for connecting with families to solicit satisfaction feedback:

- Informal check-ins during Week 1 via email or phone

- Informal check-ins via email or phone each week

- Meeting in person every 3 to 4 weeks unless an earlier meeting is requested

NOTE: The Family/Teacher Feedback form (Reproducible 3.6d) is provided as a fillable PDF in the reproducibles download (see Appendix C for download directions). While best completed when meeting in person, the PDF can be sent as an attachment via email, filled out by a family member, and returned via email. (This is recommended only for tech-savvy families.) See form in Figure 7.2b.

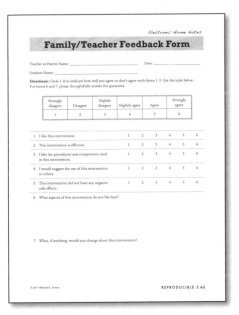

Figure 7.2b • Family/ Teacher Feedback Form

Periodically request and review family and teacher perceptions and feedback. Adjust procedures as appropriate and solicit suggestions to improve the intervention.

Family-Teacher Follow-Up and Consultation Agenda

Follow-up meetings provide an opportunity to review student progress toward goals, elicit feedback, troubleshoot any problems, and make beneficial modifications to the program. Invite family members to participate in follow-up consultation meetings every 3–4 weeks, unless the family requests a meeting earlier or pressing issues need to be addressed quickly.

Who

Meet with the family and the teacher at the same time. If this isn't possible, schedule separate meetings. Invite and include the student, if appropriate.

Summarize Information

In preparation for the follow-up meeting, summarize information from the student's chart, follow-up observation results (if the Behavior Observation Form [Reproducible 3.1a] is used), and ratings on feedback forms.

Agenda

Use the Follow-Up Consultation Meeting Agenda (Reproducible 7.2a) to guide your meeting. See Figure 7.2c on the next page.

Figure 7.2c • Follow-Up Consultation Meeting Agenda

Electronic Home Notes

Follow-Up Consultation Meeting Agenda

Teacher _____   Interventionist _____

1. Welcome and thank everyone for their cooperation and participation.

2. Review Electronic Home Note steps.

3. Review the student's ratings on the Electronic Home Notes.

4. Review academic work samples that the student has brought to Reward Days.

5. Review student satisfaction ratings.

6. Elicit family and teacher feedback.

7. Identify next steps. (Troubleshoot and adjust, or celebrate and adjust.)

8. Conclude the meeting and schedule the next consultation meeting.

© 2017 William R. Jenson

REPRODUCIBLE 7.2a

Family-Teacher Follow-Up and Consultation Meeting

1. **Welcome the student, family members, and teacher.**

   Thank everyone for participating in the program and for their willingness to work together.

2. **Review the Electronic Home Notes steps.**

   Review all that is going well. Review and model any steps that may be presenting problems. Invite questions. Troubleshoot as needed.

3. **Review the student's ratings on the Electronic Home Notes.**

   Show the student's ratings as recorded on the spreadsheet (Google Sheet) and Self-Plotting Graph. Emphasize and discuss the student's accomplishments.

4. **Review the academic work samples the student has brought to Reward Days.**

   Bring the student's work file. Show examples of the student's academic work. With the teacher's assistance, discuss the quality of work. Point out key features of the student's work that you noted when reviewing examples during Reward Days.

5. **Review the student's satisfaction ratings.**

   Share the student's responses on the feedback forms. Discuss the student's perceptions and enjoyment of the program.

6. **Elicit family and teacher feedback.**

   Ask the teacher and parents for their perceptions of the program and whether it is helping the student in class and at home. Focus on the positive feedback. Ask about any problems or barriers. Answer questions and provide clarification as necessary. *Optional:* Have participants fill out the Family/Teacher Feedback Form (Reproducible 3.6d).

7. **Identify next steps.**

Summarize student progress (or lack of progress). Then work jointly to make program and goal adjustments as needed.

- If the student has met the goals 8 out of 10 days, adjust them by increasing the expectation by 10% to 20%. Celebrate successes (see below for suggestions).

- If the student has not met the goals consistently, troubleshoot and assess program fidelity (see Section 7.3).

- If the student is meeting the goals consistently at a high level of performance, consider generalization and fading procedures (see Sections 7.4 and 7.5).

8. **Conclude the meeting and schedule the next follow-up consultation meeting.**

Arrange the next meeting. Thank the family and teacher for their time and emphasize how valuable their contributions are in helping the student be successful.

Ongoing Celebrations

Reward Days provide ongoing reinforcement for meeting goals and reviewing the Electronic Home Note with the family. In addition, special acknowledgments and periodic celebrations can boost the student's efforts. There are several ways to do this. Select options that will be reinforcing to the individual student.

- Have the student share his or her Self-Plotting Graph with the teacher, family, principal, or class.

- Write a positive note to the student, family, teacher, or principal acknowledging the student's improvement.

- Present the student with a High-Five Note (Reproducible 7.2b), On-Task Award (Reproducible 7.2c), or other award. A generic award is available as Reproducible 7.2d.

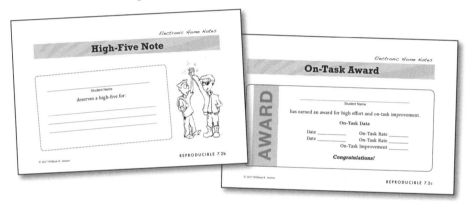

- With the student's permission, post the student's award on a "Student Accomplishments" board in the classroom or a common area like a hallway.

Cooper's Case Study, Follow-Up

Cooper's first week has gone well. Electronic Home Note procedures were followed with fidelity by all, and Cooper received high ratings. At the end of the week, Mr. James checked in with Cooper's teacher and mother. Everyone, including Cooper, was pleased with the program.

Mr. James continues to monitor Cooper's progress and program fidelity. At the end of each week, Mr. James shares Cooper's spreadsheet and graph with Ms. Anderson.

Cooper's Graph

Cooper has also been graphing his data on his Self-Plotting Graph. His graphs show ratings at a high to very high level, with a neutral trend and low bounce. This means that Cooper's response to the intervention has been immediate and consistent.

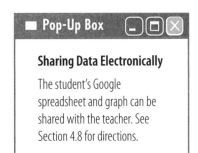

■ Pop-Up Box

Sharing Data Electronically

The student's Google spreadsheet and graph can be shared with the teacher. See Section 4.8 for directions.

Cooper's Family and Teacher Consultation Meeting

Cooper's teacher and family use his data to make evidence-based decisions. Visual analysis helps the group analyze Cooper's progress.

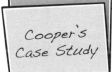

Cooper's Case Study

Cooper's Family and Teacher Consultation Meeting

Follow-Up Meeting (3 weeks)

Participants: Cooper, Mrs. West, Ms. Anderson, Mr. James

On-Task Ratings Summary: High level, neutral trend, low bounce

On-Task Goal: Goal met 14 out of 15 days, increase to all-day rating

Academic Work Samples: All assignments completed with 80%–100% accuracy

Increase Rating Time: From math only to math and reading

(continued)

Cooper's Family and Teacher Consultation Meeting (continued)

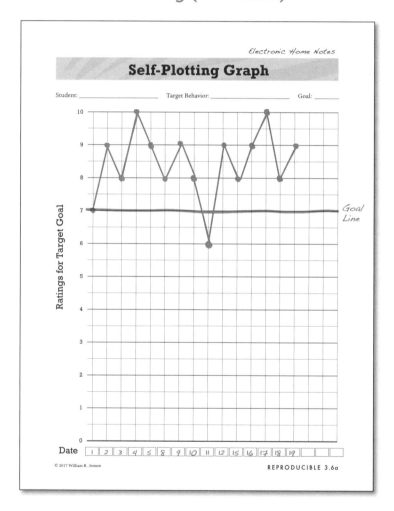

Electronic Home Notes

Self-Plotting Graph

Student: _____ Target Behavior: _____ Goal: _____

Goal Line

Date | 1 | 2 | 3 | 4 | 5 | 8 | 9 | 10 | 11 | 12 | 15 | 16 | 17 | 18 | 19 |

© 2017 William R. Jenson

REPRODUCIBLE 3.6a

Celebration: Cooper wants to share his graph with the principal. An appointment is scheduled for Monday during morning recess.

Debugging the Program
Troubleshooting

T his section provides strategies for resolving issues that may occur while using the Electronic Home Note program.

Objectives

To help problem-solve issues related to:

- Student responsibilities and follow-through
- Family follow-through and support
- Teacher follow-through and support

251

Resolving Student Behavioral Issues

What if . . .

the student does not want to participate in the program?

1. Ask why the student does not want to participate and address those concerns.

   - If the student feels singled out, consider adding a buddy.

   - Most students are not resistant to Electronic Home Notes when the intervention is presented in a positive, encouraging light with the possibility of earning rewards. To avoid this problem, present the intervention as a way to help the student succeed rather than as a form of punishment. To resolve this problem, help the student see Electronic Home Notes as a way to share successes with his or her family and learn ways to be successful.

   - Review the importance of the behavioral goals to the student's success throughout school. Explain that the behavioral goals are as important as learning how to read, write, and do math because the goals are needed on any job.

2. Once you've addressed the student's concerns, do not dwell on them. Stay focused on the procedures, the student's progress, and the rewards. Conclude the meeting on a positive note.

What if . . .

*the student is not successful in performing
the target behavior?*

1. If the student can't perform the target behavior, re-teach and practice the behavior during the Reward Day session.

2. Have the student practice the behavior in the classroom and provide frequent descriptive feedback.

3. Temporarily lower the goal or adjust when the goal is rated to increase student success.

What if . . .

*the student keeps forgetting the difference between a
target behavior (such as On Task) and misbehavior?*

1. The target behaviors may not be defined or explained clearly enough. Discuss the expectations thoroughly with the student. If necessary, model and role-play the target behaviors. Have the student practice the behaviors and check for student understanding.

2. The initial goal may be too high. Temporarily reduce the goal for a week and repeat the student training. After at least 1 week in which the student consistently receives rewards, begin to gradually increase the goal again.

What if . . .

the student consistently fails to meet behavior goals?

1. Make sure that the student is capable of meeting the goals and understands exactly what is expected.

2. Review problem areas with the student. Discuss why problems are occurring. Brainstorm ways to solve the problems and role-play the solutions with the student. Gain the student's commitment to correct the problem.

3. Reduce Electronic Home Note ratings to a single time period and gradually increase to a longer period.

4. If the student is unwilling to correct a problem, consider adding a penalty clause to the procedures. The penalty clause describes a consequence that will be delivered when criteria are not met.

What if . . .

the student's assignments show no improvement?

1. If the student shows improvement in the behavioral goals but not on assignments, informally assess whether the student has the skills to complete the assignments. For example, get a new copy of an assignment that the student had difficulty with and have the student attempt the assignment with you.

2. Ask questions. Try to determine what is preventing success. If the student has skills deficits, meet with the classroom teacher to consider modifications to assignments and additional instruction or tutoring (one-to-one or in a small group).

What if . . .

the student loses interest in participating in the program?

1. Reassess the rewards and have the student pick new ones for the Reward Menu.

2. Set up a meeting with the student's family and teacher to discuss possible reasons for lack of motivation.

3. The reward payoff may be too delayed. Cut the time needed to earn the reward in half.

What if . . .

the student's difficulties seem due in part to a skill deficit (i.e., Can't Do) rather than a lack of motivation (i.e., Won't Do)?

1. An appropriate approach to teaching Tough Kids involves planning and implementing the behavior management techniques they require while teaching them the academic skills they need. Without improvement in academic skills, even the most advanced behavior management system will not improve desired behaviors in the long term. Additional or adapted instruction should be provided by increasing the student's academic learning time and matching academic tasks with the student's ability levels.

2. By definition, Tough Kids exhibit significant social skills deficits when compared with their successful peers. When Tough Kids have not acquired necessary social skills vicariously, they must be taught directly, with a focus on specific problem areas. Teach behaviors that will maximize success and minimize failure. Teach behaviors that are needed and will be used in other settings. Provide opportunities

for role-play, rehearsal, and supervised practice. Use periodic booster sessions if the student's behavior deteriorates or as a preventive measure. Re-teach or review appropriate lessons. (See *The Tough Kid Social Skills Book* in Resources at the back of the book.)

3. Reduce the goal to the student's current level of performance (e.g., a goal of 60%) and gradually increase as academic supports are added.

What if . . .

the student argues with you about a rating?

1. Explain to the student that the teacher is like a referee in a game such as football, baseball, or basketball. The players cannot argue but need to accept the referee's decisions. This is called good sportsmanship. Tell the student you will not explain again and that arguing will lower the rating.

2. Provide positive descriptive feedback when the student problem-solves low ratings with you. Send a positive note to the parent when the student works responsibly to make improvements.

3. Let parents know that you are working on good sportsmanship when a rating is low and ask them to use low ratings as an opportunity to discuss how to make improvements.

Resolving Issues With Family Follow-Through and Support

What if . . .

the family is unwilling to participate or views the procedures as a negative judgment about their parenting abilities?

This problem can usually be circumvented by conducting the preliminary Family and Teacher Meeting (Section 5.3). However, should it occur after a positive meeting, consider the following solutions.

1. Meet with the student's family, discuss student improvements, and address any concerns they may have with the Electronic Home Note program. Make sure the family understands that the purpose of the Electronic Home Note program is to provide support and not to punish the student. Explain that Electronic Home Notes will be used to help the student be more on task and work more efficiently, and to provide positive feedback about the student's behavior at school.

2. Ask the parent to try the program for a 2-week trial period.

3. If the parents still do not want to participate, tell them that you would like to use the Electronic Home Note with another staff member monitoring (e.g., counselor, special education teacher). If that's successful, you can meet again to see if the family would like to participate in the Electronic Home Note program.

What if . . .

you suspect the family may deliver excessively punishing consequences for poor performance?

1. Meet with the family and ask for their cooperation in delivering predetermined positive feedback and, if necessary, mildly aversive consequences.

2. Help the parent understand that if aversive consequences are too severe, the student will likely not make progress and may begin to have more problems at school.

3. If you believe the aversive consequences are too severe, consider a different intervention.

What if . . .

the parent does not regularly review the Electronic Home Note?

1. Connect with the family. Provide positive descriptive feedback about the student's enthusiasm when the family completed a review and reply and the student earned a Reward Day.

   Help the family identify a time when they can consistently review the Electronic Home Note with their child.

2. Socially reinforce the student for taking the initiative and prompting the parent to review the note. For example, say to the student something like: *I really appreciate it when you ask your parents to review the note. It really helps me. It shows that you are being very responsible.*

3. If the family does not review the note or is inconsistent, call the student in on the scheduled Reward Day and ask: *Did you try to get your parents to review the note?* If the student says that he or she did ask, include the student in the Reward Day with the other students. If this continues to be a problem, you may have to arrange for another person in the school (e.g., an aide, counselor, or teacher) to act as a surrogate parent to review the note with the student.

Resolving Issues With a Teacher's Follow-Through and Support

What if . . .

the teacher is hesitant to use the program because it gives a disproportionate amount of attention to the student referred for intervention as compared with other students?

1. During the Teacher Consultation and Training Meeting, discuss with the teacher the necessity of providing each student with what he or she needs to have an equal chance of success. If Tough Kids are highly unmotivated because of years of academic failure, they will need external incentive systems to keep them motivated as they acquire necessary academic and behavioral skills.

2. Make sure the teacher understands that the purpose of the Electronic Home Note program is to help the student be more on task and work more efficiently, and that the program will be used to provide feedback about the student's behaviors at school.

What if . . .

the teacher forgets to submit the Electronic Home Note?

1. Problem-solve with the teacher. Identify times when the teacher can send the Electronic Home Note reliably (e.g., if after school is not a consistently good time due to meetings and other responsibilities, suggest sending the Electronic Home Note during afternoon recess).

2. Tell the teacher you are happy to provide prompts (e.g., notes on the teacher's computer or mailbox, daily check-ins).

What if . . .

the teacher's behavior ratings are inconsistent?

1. Intervention procedures may not be defined or explained clearly enough. Check to see that definitions of target behaviors are clear enough to rate consistently.

2. Repeat the teacher training. Discuss the intervention steps and responsibilities thoroughly with the teacher.

3. Conduct follow-up observations or conduct side-by-side ratings with the teacher so you can compare and discuss ratings on student behaviors. (e.g., a teacher may underestimate compliance because the student did not follow one direction out of ten.)

4. Have the teacher practice rating the student and check for understanding.

Going Viral

Generalization

As students consistently achieve their individualized goals and demonstrate desired behaviors at levels similar to their peers, consider focusing on skill transfer, fading procedures, and celebrating student success. This section focuses on generalization, or skill transfer.

Objective

To increase generalization of target behaviors across longer periods of time

Procedures for Generalizing Skills

Skill transfer should focus on the student's use of desired target behaviors in a variety of settings with a variety of people and across a variety of times. There are several methods to enhance generalization.

- **Gradually increase the length of the Electronic Home Note rating period.**

  Increase the length of time that the student is expected to demonstrate appropriate behaviors. For example, increase the length of a rating period from 15 minutes to 30 minutes or from 30 minutes to an hour.

- **Gradually increase the number of rating periods.**

  Use the Electronic Home Note to rate the student's target behaviors across a variety of different times or class periods. For example, track the student's behavior during reading, math, and writing instead of just math.

Pop-Up Box

The Tough Kid On-Task in a Box

This program includes procedures for improving on-task rates for the whole class as well as for a single student or buddies. See the Resources section at the end of the book.

Next Step • Self-Monitoring

Self-monitoring can be used to increase the effectiveness of an Electronic Home Notes intervention by helping the student become aware of his or her own behaviors. This procedure can be added to the Electronic Home Notes intervention to help generalize the behavior or as the intervention is faded.

NOTE: For students with an on-task goal, consider using the self-monitoring tools and procedures from *The Tough Kid On-Task in a Box*.

Self-Monitoring Form

Alternatively, have the student use the Self-Monitoring Form (Reproducible 7.4a) shown in Figure 7.4a. Fill in the student's goal or goals. Underline the target goal rating (e.g., 4 or 5). Start by teaching the student to rate only the priority goal. When comparing the student's ratings with the teacher's, use the following key:

Teacher Ratings	Student Rating
0–2 (0% to 20%)	1 (Very Poor: Rarely)
3–4 (30% to 40%)	2 (Poor: Not very often)
5–6 (50% to 60%)	3 (Below Average: Sometimes)
7–8 (70% to 80%)	4 (Average: Mostly)
9–10 (90% to 100%)	5 (Exceptional: Always)

Figure 7.4a • Self-Monitoring Form

Electronic Home Notes

Self-Monitoring Form

Student _George Jackson_   Date _5/18_

Teacher _Martha Jones_

Student Goal	Rating				
Stay on Task	1	2	3	(4)	5
Follow Directions	1	2	3	4	(5)
KYH/FOOTY	1	2	3	4	(5)
	1	2	3	4	5
	1	2	3	4	5

Rating Scale—Circle a Number

1 = Very Poor (Rarely)
2 = Poor (Not very often)
3 = Below Average (Sometimes)
4 = Average (Mostly)
5 = Exceptional (Always)

Teacher Rating Scale

1 = Rating 0–2
2 = Rating 3–4
3 = Rating 5–6
4 = Rating 7–8
5 = Rating 9–10

If the teacher agrees with the student rating, put a line across the circled rating. ⊘
If the teacher disagrees with the student rating, put an "x" across the circled rating. ⊗

Comments:

© 2017 William R. Jenson   REPRODUCIBLE 7.4a

Self-Monitoring Sessions

1. **Meet with the student for a special training session.**

   - Introduce the self-monitoring form.

   - Go over the target behavior, the definition of the target behavior, and the rating goal.
     Check for understanding by asking questions like:

     What does [keep your hands, feet and other objects to yourself] *look like during PE?*

     What does [keep your hands, feet and other objects to yourself] *look like when you are changing groups?*

     What is your goal for your Reward Day? (Always)

2. **Have the student practice rating his or her behavior during the same time period as the teacher.**

3. **Have the student and teacher compare ratings.**

   Have the teacher and student discuss their ratings. Provide positive descriptive feedback when ratings are for the same category. For example, say things like: *Wow, your rating was very close to the teacher's. You both said you "mostly" followed directions right away.*

   Discuss any differences. For example, ask the student things like: *Hmm, you said you "always followed directions" (9–10), but the teacher's rating indicates just "sometimes" (6). Let's think about what your teacher saw and you did.*

   When it was time to clean up, did you clean up right away? (No, I wanted to play with the trucks a little bit more.)

Did you go to your reading group right away when the teacher called you? (yes)
I would agree. Did you open up your book to the right page? (yes)
Oops, the teacher had to help you because you were daydreaming.
So, do you think you "always" followed directions right away?
Thank you for thinking about your goal with me. You are going to get really good at self-monitoring.

4. **Repeat the practice sessions until the student is able to reliably self-monitor the target behavior.**

   Reinforce the student for participating by allowing an extra spin of the spinner on Reward Days and providing the reward.

5. **Determine when the student should self-monitor. Establish this as a routine with the classroom teacher's support.**

   In general, the student should self-monitor during the same time period that the teacher is rating the student. If the teacher is rating the student over a long period of time (a half day to a full day), have the student self-monitor during a challenging period of the day.

6. **Reward the student for self-monitoring when it is added to the routine.**

   On Reward Days, you can select from the following types of options for reinforcing self-monitoring. You might reward the student for:

   - Using the Self-Recording Form
   - Correctly rating the target behavior
   - Meeting the target goal

Cooper's Case Study, Self-Monitoring

Mr. James suggests that Cooper and a buddy (also on Electronic Home Notes) start working in *The Tough Kid On-Task in a Box* program. (See Resources at the end of the book.)

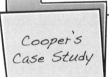

Cooper's Case Study

Self-Monitoring

Follow-Up Meeting (8 weeks)

Participants: Cooper, Mrs. West, Ms. Anderson, Mr. James

On-Task Ratings Summary: Maintaining high levels of success in math and reading

Academic Work Samples: All math assignments completed with 80%–100% accuracy; reading work completed with 90%–100% accuracy; fluency scores improving; needs work on handwriting

Add: Self-monitoring with On-Task in a Box
Cooper will work with a buddy in the On-Task in a Box program. Self-monitoring will begin after a 2-week orientation period with his buddy.

Going Offline

Fade the Program

As the student consistently meets the goals and demonstrates the desired target behaviors, both at a level similar to that of peers and in a variety of settings, begin fading the program. Generally speaking, the Electronic Home Note program should be used every day, with Reward Days provided two to three times per week, across 8 weeks. In general, begin fading the program when the student exhibits the desired target behaviors for at least 8 of 10 days at a rate similar to peers (e.g., 80% for on-task behavior).

Options for Fading

There are several options for fading use of the Electronic Home Note program.

1. **Increase the time between the Electronic Home Note rating periods each day.**

   Use fewer ratings over longer periods of time. For example, use one Electronic Home Note rating over an entire day.

2. **Increase the interval between Electronic Home Notes.**

   Reduce the frequency at which the Electronic Home Note is sent to the family. For example, the teacher might send the Electronic Home

■ **Pop-Up Box**

Ongoing Maintenance

Some students with chronic or severe behavior problems may revert to undesirable behavior if the program ends. For these students, use the Electronic Home Note program as an ongoing maintenance program.

Note on random days, once a week, or every Monday, Wednesday and Friday.

3. **Reduce the frequency of Reward Days.**

   Reduce how often a student is rewarded for desired target behavior by having the Reward Days occur less frequently but still unpredictably. For example, you might have a Reward Day on Wednesday one week and the next week on Tuesday, Thursday, and Friday.

4. **Increase the number of required moves on the Chart Moves Board.**

   Maintain the frequency of Reward Days, but increase the amount of time between earning highly valued rewards on the Chart Moves Board. For example, use a board with 30 squares instead of 15 (see Reproducible 7.5a).

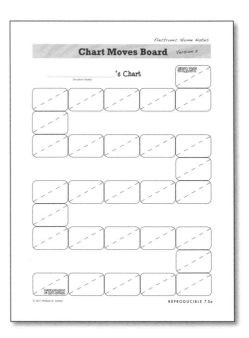

5. **Use more social (vs. tangible) rewards.**

   Instead of material rewards, transition the student to earning more socially reinforcing activities. For example, offer rewards like extra time at recess with a friend or the opportunity to be a teacher or peer helper.

Cooper's Case Study, New Semester

At 12 weeks into the Electronic Home Notes intervention, Cooper is still demonstrating high rates of success. Because Cooper has a long history of challenging behavior in the classroom, Ms. Anderson and Cooper's family decide to maintain the Electronic Home Note intervention for the remainder of the school year.

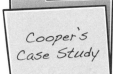

Cooper's Case Study

Cooper's End-of-Semester Report

Follow-Up Meeting (end of semester)

Participants: Cooper, Mrs. West, Ms. Anderson, Mr. James

On-Task Ratings Summary: Maintaining high levels of success in math and reading

Self-Monitoring: Going well, running booster sessions once every two weeks

Academic Work Samples

Math: Cooper's work samples consistently reflect 80% to 100% accuracy in math, reflecting strong math skills.

Reading: Cooper's fluency is above average for his age level; oral comprehension is strong.

Writing: Handwriting continues to be a struggle. On-task rates are lower when work requires writing.

At the end of the semester, the group creates a new home note with new and more sophisticated goals. Mr. James is able to meet with Cooper for less frequent Reward Days.

Cooper's Case Study, End-of-Year Recommendations

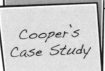

Cooper's Case Study

Cooper's End-of-Year Report

Follow-Up Meeting (end of year)

Participants: Cooper, Mrs. West, Ms. Anderson, Mr. James

Cooper has had a stellar year, with improvements to the level of his peers in on-task behavior, following directions, staying in his seat, and appropriate voice level.

Homework completion has also improved to rates similar to his peers.

Recommendation for fifth grade: Start the year with an Electronic Home Note and Reward Day to get the year off to a positive start. Cooper has expressed an interest in being an on-task tutor for younger students.

Achenbach, T. M., & Rescorla, L. A. (2001). *Manual for the ASEBA School-Age Forms & Profiles*. Burlington, VT: University of Vermont, Research Center for Children, Youth, & Families.

Adams, M. B., Womack, S. A., Shatzer, R. H., & Caldarella, P. (2010). Parent involvement in school-wide social skills instruction: Perceptions of a home note program. *Education, 130,* 513–528.

Atkeson, B. M., & Forehand, R. (1979). Home-based reinforcement programs designed to modify classroom behavior: A review and methodological evaluation. *Psychological Bulletin, 86,* 1298–1308.

Bailey, J. S., Wolf, M. M., & Phillips, E. L. (1970). Home-based reinforcement and the modification of pre-delinquents' classroom behavior. *Journal of Applied Behavior Analysis, 3,* 223–233.

Blechman, E. A., Taylor, C. J., & Schrader, S. M. (1981). Family problem solving versus home notes as early intervention with high-risk children. *Journal of Consulting and Clinical Psychology, 49,* 919–926.

Budd, K. S., Leibowitz, J. M., Riner, L. S., Mindell, C., & Goldfarb, A. L. (1981). Home-based treatment of severe disruptive behaviors: A reinforcement package for preschool and kindergarten children. *Behavior Modification, 5,* 273–298.

Chafouleas, S. M., Riley-Tillman, T. C., & Sassu, K. A. (2006). Acceptability and reported use of daily behavior report cards among teachers. *Journal of Positive Behavior Interventions, 8*(3), 174–182.

Chafouleas, S. M., Riley-Tillman, T. C., & Christ, T. J. (2009). Direct behavior rating (DBR): An emerging method for assessing social behavior within a tiered intervention system. *Assessment for Effective Intervention, 34,* 195–200.

references

Conners, K. (2008). *Comprehensive behavior rating scales* (3rd ed.). North Tonawanda, NY: Multi-Health Systems.

Dougherty, E. H., & Dougherty, A. (1977). The daily report card: A simplified and flexible package for classroom management. *Psychology in the Schools, 14*(2), 191–195.

Drew, B. M., Evans, J. H., Bostow, D. E., Geiger, G., & Drash, P. N. (1982). Increasing assignment completion and accuracy using a daily report card procedure. *Psychology in the Schools, 19,* 540–547.

Edlund, C. V. (1969). Rewards at home to promote desirable school behavior. *Teaching Exceptional Children, 1*(4), 121–127.

Fabiano, G. A., Vujnovic, R. K., Pelham, W. E., Waschbusch, D. A., Massetti, G. M., Pariseau, M. E., Naylor, J., Yu, J., Robins, M., Carnefix, T., Greiner, A. R., & Volker, M. (2010). Enhancing the effectiveness of special education programming for children with attention-deficit/hyperactivity disorder using a daily report card. *School Psychology Review, 39*(2), 219–239.

Frafjord-Jacobson, K. L., Hanson, A. C., McLaughlin, T. F., Stansell, A., & Howard, V. F. (2013). Daily report card: A recommended intervention in the schools. *International Journal of Basics and Applied Sciences, 1,* 461–472.

Galloway, J., & Sheridan, S. M. (1994). Implementing scientific practices through case studies: Examples using home-school interventions and consultation. *Journal of School Psychology, 32,* 385–413.

Jenson, W. R., Bowen, J., Clark, E., Block, H., Gabrielsen, T., Hood, J., Radley, K., & Springer, B. (2011). *Superheroes Social Skills* [multimedia program]. Eugene, OR: Pacific Northwest Publishing.

Jenson, W. R., Rhode, G., & Reavis, K. (2009). *The Tough Kid tool box.* Eugene, OR: Pacific Northwest Publishing.

Jenson, W. R., & Sprick, M. (2014). *The Tough Kid on-task in a box.* Eugene, OR: Pacific Northwest Publishing.

Johnson, K. R. (2008). *A comparison of home and school-based reinforcement of home notes.* (Unpublished doctoral dissertation). University of Utah, Salt Lake City, UT.

Jurbergs, N., Palcic, J., & Kelley, M. L. (2007). School-home notes with and without response cost: Increasing attention and academic performance in low-income children with Attention-Deficit/Hyperactivity Disorder. *School Psychology Quarterly, 22,* 358–379.

Jurbergs, N., Palcic, J. L., & Kelley, M. L. (2010). Daily behavior report cards with and without home-based consequences: Improving behavior in low income, African American children with ADHD. *Child and Family Behavior Therapy, 32*(3), 177–195.

Kelley, M. L. (1990). *School-home notes: Promoting children's classroom success.* New York, NY: Guilford Press.

Knorr, J. M. (2015). *A validation and efficacy study examining the electronic home note intervention package for increasing rates of on-task and academic performance.* (Unpublished doctoral dissertation). University of Utah, Department of Educational Psychology, Salt Lake City, UT.

Leach, D. J., & Byrne, M. K. (1986). Some 'spill-over' effects of a home-based reinforcement programme in a secondary school. *Educational Psychology, 6,* 265–276.

LeBel, T. J., Chafouleas, S. M., Britner, P. A., & Simonsen, B. (2012). Use of a daily behavior report card in an intervention package involving home-school communication to reduce disruptive behavior in preschoolers. *Journal of Positive Behavior Interventions, 15*(2), 103–112.

Lopach, L. C. (2016). *The electronic daily school note: A study examining an evidence-based school intervention package for improving on-task behavior, academics, and home-school collaboration* (Unpublished doctoral dissertation). University of Utah, Department of Educational Psychology, Salt Lake City, UT.

McCain, A. P., & Kelley, M. L. (1993). Managing the classroom behavior of an ADHD preschooler: The efficacy of a school-home note intervention. *Child and Behavior Therapy, 15*(3), 33–44.

McGoey, K. E., Prodan, T., & Condit, N. (2007). Examining the effects of teacher and self-evaluation of disruptive behaviors via school-home notes for two young children in kindergarten. *Journal of Early and Intensive Behavior Intervention, 3*(1), 365–376.

Owens, J. S., Holdaway, A. S., Zoromski, A. K., Evans, S. W., Himawan, L. K., Girio-Herrera, E., & Murphy, C. E. (2012). Incremental benefits of a daily report card intervention over time for youth with disruptive behavior. *Behavior Therapy, 43*, 848–861.

Reynolds, C. R., & Kamphaus, R. (2015). *BASC-3 Behavioral and Emotional Screening System* (BASC-3 BESS). San Antonio, TX: Pearson.

Rhode, G., Jenson, W. R., & Reavis, K. (2010). *The Tough Kid book: Practical classroom strategies* (2nd ed.). Eugene, OR: Pacific Northwest Publishing.

Riley-Tillman, T. C., Chafouleas, S. M., & Briesch, A. M. (2007). A school practitioner's guide to using daily behavior report cards to monitor student behavior. *Psychology in the Schools, 44*(1), 77–89.

Riley-Tillman, T. C., Chafouleas, S. M., Briesch, A. M., & Eckert, T. L. (2008). Daily behavior report cards and systematic direct observation: An investigation of the acceptability, reported training and use, and decision reliability among school psychologists. *Journal of Behavior Education, 17*(4), 313–327.

Schumaker, J. B., Hovell, M. F., & Sherman, J. A. (1977). An analysis of daily report cards and parent-managed privileges in the improvement of adolescents' classroom performance. *Journal of Applied Behavior Analysis, 10*(3), 449–464.

Sheridan, S. M. (2003, April). *Home/school/community collaboration: Connections for kids.* Invited address at the annual meeting of the National Association of School Psychologists, Toronto, Canada.

Trovato, J., & Bucher, B. (1980). Peer tutoring with or without home-based reinforcement, for reading remediation. *Journal of Applied Behavior Analysis, 13*(1), 129–141.

Tugend, A. (March, 23, 2012). *Praise is fleeting, but brickbats we recall.* The New York Times, p. B5.

Vannest, K. J., Davis, J. L., Davis, C. R., Mason, B. A., & Burke, M. D. (2010). Effective intervention for behavior with a daily behavior report card: A meta-analysis. *School Psychology Review, 39*(4), 654–672.

Volpe, R. J., & Fabiano, G. A. (2013). *Daily behavior report cards: An evidence based system of assessment and intervention.* New York, NY: Guilford Press.

Practice Making Electronic Home Notes

If you've never set up an Electronic Home Note, it will take about an hour to practice. Each time you create one, it becomes easier and faster. Eventually, it will take only a few minutes to set up each new Electronic Home Note and spreadsheet. This appendix includes directions for interventionists and a separate set of directions for teacher-interventionists. **NOTE:** Be sure to give each practice file a different name.

Directions for Interventionists

Complete the directions in each of the following sections. It is very important to follow every direction. *Do not skip anything or change the order of steps.*

As you read **Section 4.1**, note that you will be taking the role of the interventionist.

Section 4.2: How to Get Started With Google

Keep a record of your dedicated Electronic Home Notes Google username and password. You will use your new dedicated Google account to practice setting up the Electronic Home Note.

Section 4.3: How to Create an Electronic Home Note

Information needed to complete this section:

- Create the home note for a student named Amanda

- Teacher's email address: *For practice purposes, use your school email address.*

- Parent's email address: *For practice purposes, use your personal email address so you can see what the parents receive.*

NOTE: You will need three email addresses to practice: one for you the interventionist, one for the teacher's role, and one for the parent's role.

- For each behavior (1, 2, 3, etc.), enter the following:

  Behavior 1. On Task
  Description: Maintain eye contact with the teacher or task, and perform only the requested task, math independent work

  Behavior 2. Follow Directions
  Description: Follow a staff member's directions in 3 to 5 seconds

  Behavior 3. Stay in Seat
  Description: Remain in seat. Leave only if requested or required (getting materials)

  Behavior 4. Appropriate Voice Level
  Description: Use a voice level appropriate to the classroom activity

Section 4.4: How to Set Up a Spreadsheet and Automate the Email

Section 4.5b: Next Steps for Interventionists

Section 4.6: How to Set Up Reward Day Notifications for the Student

Section 4.7: How to Create a Chart in Google Sheets (Optional)

NOTE: To practice creating a chart, you will need at least two data points. Plan to send practice Electronic Home Notes to your parent email across two days. Then set up a chart.

Section 4.8: How to Share the Spreadsheet Information (Optional)

NOTE: If you wish to practice again, create an Electronic Home Note and spreadsheet for a student named Amanda 2.

Section 4.9: How to Organize Your Documents

Directions for Teacher-Interventionists

It is very important to follow every direction. *Do not skip anything or change the order of directions.*

As you read **Section 4.1**, note that you will be taking the role of the teacher-interventionist.

Section 4.2: How to Get Started With Google

Keep a record of your dedicated Electronic Home Notes Google username and password. You will use your new dedicated Google account to practice setting up an Electronic Home Note.

Section 4.3: How to Create an Electronic Home Note

Information needed to complete this section:

- Create the home note for a student named Amanda

- Parent's email address: *For practice purposes, use your school or personal email address so you can see what the parents receive.*

  NOTE: You will need two email addresses to practice: one for you, the teacher-interventionist (dedicated Google account), and one for the parent's role.

- For each behavior (1, 2, 3, etc.), enter the following:

  Behavior 1. On Task
  Description: Maintain eye contact with the teacher or task, and perform only the requested task, math independent work

  Behavior 2. Follow Directions
  Description: Follow a staff member's directions in 3 to 5 seconds

Behavior 3. Stay in Seat
Description: Remain in seat. Leave only if requested or required (getting materials

Behavior 4. Appropriate Voice Level
Description: Use a voice level appropriate to the classroom activity

Section 4.4 : How to Set Up a Spreadsheet and Automate the Email

Section 4.5a: Next Steps for Teacher-Interventionists

Section 4.6: How to Set Up Reward Day Notifications for the Student

Section 4.7: How to Create a Chart in Google Sheets (Optional)

NOTE: To practice creating a chart, you will need at least two data points. Plan to send practice Electronic Home Notes to your parent email across two days. Then set up a chart.

Section 4.8: How to Share Data and Personalize the Electronic Home Note (Optional)

NOTE: If you wish to practice again, create an Electronic Home Note and spreadsheet for a student named Amanda 2.

Using a Traditional Paper Home Note

Traditional paper home notes are associated with a number of drawbacks, such as notes being forgotten, lost, destroyed, or even forged. However, if an Electronic Home Note is not a viable option, sending home a paper home note is the next best thing.

Objective

To apply the steps in creating and implementing Electronic Home Notes to the use of a paper home note

Although there are many options (formats and procedures) for putting together a viable paper home note program, this appendix provides a quick guide for applying the procedures in the Electronic Home Note program to a paper home note program. See the Electronic Home Note and paper home note in Figure B.1 on the next page.

Though procedurally a paper home note follows the same steps, there are three major differences between a paper and an Electronic Home Note.

1. The student is responsible for taking the home note home, getting it signed, and bringing it back to school the next day.

2. Automated notification of unpredictable Reward Days is replaced by a different messaging system.

3. Automated data collection of student ratings is replaced with a different record-keeping system.

Figure B.1 • Electronic Home Note and Paper Home Note

Home Note Form

TEACHER NAME

* Required

Parent's Email *

○ ENTER PARENT EMAIL

BEHAVIOR 1 *
Description of Behavior

	0	1	2	3	4	5	6	7	8	9	10
Never	○	○	○	○	○	○	○	○	○	○	○	Always

BEHAVIOR 2 *
Description of Behavior

	0	1	2	3	4	5	6	7	8	9	10
Never	○	○	○	○	○	○	○	○	○	○	○	Always

BEHAVIOR 3 *
Description of Behavior

	0	1	2	3	4	5	6	7	8	9	10
Never	○	○	○	○	○	○	○	○	○	○	○	Always

BEHAVIOR 4 *
Description of Behavior

	0	1	2	3	4	5	6	7	8	9	10
Never	○	○	○	○	○	○	○	○	○	○	○	Always

BEHAVIOR 5 *
Description of Behavior

	0	1	2	3	4	5	6	7	8	9	10
Never	○	○	○	○	○	○	○	○	○	○	○	Always

Comments

Your answer

SUBMIT

Never submit passwords through Google Forms.

Electronic Home Notes

Home Note

Name _____ Date _____

Directions: Please circle the student's rating. Never = 0, Always = 10.

Behavior	Rating
1	0 1 2 3 4 5 6 7 8 9 10
2	0 1 2 3 4 5 6 7 8 9 10
3	0 1 2 3 4 5 6 7 8 9 10
4	0 1 2 3 4 5 6 7 8 9 10
5	0 1 2 3 4 5 6 7 8 9 10

Comments:

Teacher Initials _____ Parent Initials _____
Please rate and sign in ink.

© 2017 William R. Jenson

REPRODUCIBLE B.1

The following steps provide a general outline for setting up and implementing a paper home note system.

Step 1. Read Sections 3.1 to 3.4.

Section 3 provides all the how-to information needed to:

- Assess student behavior
- Identify appropriate target behaviors
- Set up behavior scaling and goals
- Set up an effective motivational system, including unpredictable Reward Days

Step 2. Read Sections 5.1 through 5.5.

The procedures in Section 5 provide important information on:

- Initial connections with the teacher and family
- Consultation and training with the teacher
- Consultation and training with the family and teacher
- Consultation and training with the student
- Follow-up observations

Follow the procedures in Section 5, omitting procedures that are specific to Electronic Home Notes. In addition, before meeting with the student, make sure all procedures for taking the paper home note home, reviewing it, and bringing it back have been worked out with the teacher and family.

Suggestions include:

1. Determine with the teacher how and when he or she will give the home note to the student (e.g., the teacher will give the student the home note while students are in line to go home, and the student will immediately put the note in his backpack). Keep in mind that the teacher will also need a brief amount of time to mark the note at the end of the day.

2. Determine with the family member when the home note will be reviewed (e.g., as soon as the student gets home, right after dinner, etc.).

3. Determine with the family member where the home note will be put after reviewing it so it isn't forgotten in the morning (e.g., the family puts the note in the student's backpack as soon as he or she signs it).

Electronic Home Notes also include an automated Reward Day notification. Before meeting with the family, determine with the teacher how the student will turn in the signed home note and learn about Reward Days. (See Section 6 for how to schedule unpredictable Reward Days.) Some options follow:

- The student reports to the interventionist's office before going to class and turns in the signed home note. As indicated by the unpredictable Reward Day schedule, the interventionist hangs a sign on the door announcing "REWARD DAY."

- The interventionist shares the unpredictable Reward Day schedule with the teacher (who promises to keep the schedule a secret). The student turns in the signed home note to the teacher, and the teacher lets the student know when it's a Reward Day or gives the student a Reward Day notification (Reproducible B.2).

- The interventionist puts a Reward Day notification in the teacher's box on Reward Days. As soon as the student enters the classroom, the student gives the signed home note to the teacher. The teacher then gives the Reward Day notification to the student.

NOTE: If the teacher collects the signed home notes, the interventionist will need a procedure for collecting them and recording the behavioral ratings.

Step 3. Read Sections 6.1–6.3.

This section provides information on how to conduct a Reward Day (whether using a paper or an Electronic Home Note). This section also explains how to teach the student to use a Self-Plotting graph. Self-plotting graphs can serve a dual function—to help the student take ownership of his or her progress and to provide all parties with a visual record of the student's progress.

Step 4. Read Section 7.

In this final section of the manual, you will learn how to monitor the student's responsiveness to the intervention and make data-based decisions with all the stakeholders—student, family, and classroom teacher.

Troubleshooting (specific to paper home notes)

What if . . .

the student loses, forgets, destroys, or forges the home note?

Do not accept excuses. Prearrange reductive consequences (those that reduce rather than increase the behavior) that can be implemented consistently, firmly, and in a neutral tone or fashion. A reductive consequence can be given at home or at school and may include the loss of a privilege. For example, the student might lose computer time at home or school.

Concurrently, reinforce the student with motivating consequences when he or she follows the home note procedures. Make Reward Days fun, and encourage the family and teacher to acknowledge the student's progress.

Index of Reproducible Forms

The purchaser is granted permission to use and reproduce the reproducible forms in this book and available for download solely for use in
implementing *The Tough Kid Electronic Home Notes* program as described
in this book. Except as expressly permitted above and under the United
States Copyright Act of 1976, no materials in this work may be used,
reproduced, or distributed in any form or by any means, electronic or
mechanical, without the prior written permission of the publisher.

All forms are available to download online. Go to: cdcontent.pacificnw
publish.com and enter access code 978-1-59909-085-6. Forms are provided
in PDF format. Below is a list of forms with corresponding reproducible
numbers and location in the book.

List of Reproducible Forms

The Tough Kid Series

Books and programs in The Tough Kid Series can help you manage and motivate Tough Kids, in the school setting. You will learn practical, evidence-based strategies for dealing with tough problems like aggression, noncompliance, lack of motivation, and poor academic performance.

Call **1-866-542-1490** or shop online
at **www.PacificNWPublish.com**

FOR GRADES
1 - 6

The Tough Kid On-Task in a Box

William R. Jenson, Ph.D., and Marilyn Sprick, M.S.

The Tough Kid On-Task in a Box employs the research-baed strategies of self-monitoring, self-graphing, and video peer modeling. The program helped students improve time on task from a baseline average of 32% to 88%. At follow-up, students had an average on-task rate of 85% in their regular classrooms.

The Tough Kid Book (2nd ed.)

Ginger Rhode, Ph.D., William R. Jenson, Ph.D., and H. Kenton Reavis, Ed.D.

FOR GRADES
1 - 8

The original Tough Kid book is updated with creative techniques that you can use immediately to deal with tough classroom behaviors such as aggression, noncompliance, tantrums, and more. The book covers positive procedures that reward desired student behavior as well as reductive techniques that stop problem behaviors.

The Tough Kid Tool Box

William R. Jenson, Ph.D., Ginger Rhode, Ph.D., and H. Kenton Reavis, Ed.D.

No teacher should be without these practical tools for classroom behavior management. *The Tough Kid Tool Box* provides an assortment of materials you can use to quickly implement behavior management strategies. Ready-to-print reproducibles are provided in both English and Spanish.

The Tough Kid Teachers and Parents as Partners

Susan M. Sheridan, Ph.D.

The Tough Kid Teachers and Parents as Partners (TAPP) provides strategies for building positive, collaborative relationships with parents that benefit all students, and a process for dealing with those more challenging students—Tough Kids.

The Tough Kid Social Skills Book

Susan M. Sheridan, Ph.D.

When students don't know how to resolve conflict, express frustration, or interact with others, they have difficulty with schoolwork and in their personal lives. This Tough Kid volume addresses ten specific social skills, including dealing with teasing, using self-control, solving arguments, and joining in.